A TOXIC DIVIDE

The Hidden Toll of Environmental Racism in America

Dr. Crystal Chavis

Copyright © 2025 by Crystal D. Chavis

All rights reserved. No part of this publication may be reproduced, distributed, or transmitted in any form or by any means, including photocopying, recording, or any other electronic or mechanical methods, without the prior written permission of the publisher, except in the case of brief quotations embodied in critical reviews and certain other noncommercial uses permitted by copyright law.

First Edition

Published in the United States by Chavis Press, Baltimore, Maryland.

Hardcover ISBN: 979-8-9938227-0-9

Paperback ISBN: 979-8-9938227-1-6

eBook ISBN: 979-8-9938227-2-3

LCCN: 2025923540

DISCLAIMER

THIS BOOK IS A work of nonfiction based on research, public records, and personal interviews. While every effort has been made to verify the accuracy of the information presented, the author and publisher assume no responsibility for errors, omissions, or the outcomes of actions taken based on the information contained herein.

The views and interpretations expressed are those of the author and do not necessarily reflect those of any organization, institution, or individual referenced or acknowledged. Some names and identifying details of individuals have been changed to protect their privacy.

This work is provided for informational and educational purposes only and is not intended as legal, medical, or professional advice.

DEDICATION

To my grandfather
Your belief in me is my foundation.
This work carries the echoes of your faith.

FOREWORD

By John Beard Jr.

Founder and CEO,
Port Arthur Community Action Network

Life in America during the 2020s feels like trying to fly a kite in a hurricane. The pace and intensity of change are relentless, shaking the very foundations of what we know, believe, and accept. The earth beneath our feet and the air we breathe seem to be transforming in ways we never imagined, touching every aspect of our lives.

My journey as an advocate has been shaped by what I believe were preordained steps. Rooted in family and faith, I've always felt a calling to serve the greater good, especially within communities of color that have long been entangled in the oil and gas industry. I was born and raised on the "fenceline," just steps from tank farms and in the shadows of some of the world's largest petrochemical facilities. I spent thirty-eight years working in the oil industry, following in the footsteps of my father as a second-generation laborer and union member. I also served three terms on the Port Arthur City Council and as mayor pro tem.

In 2014, everything changed. A predominantly Black neighborhood was exposed to a benzene release. While the city profited millions, the affected community—thousands of people—received only $350,000. That injustice lit a fire in me. Though our fight for a fairer deal fell short, it led to the founding of PACAN (Port Arthur Community Action Network), an organization committed to helping everyday people confront pollution, poverty, hurricanes, and systemic injustice.

It was through this work that I met Dr. Crystal Chavis. While researching her doctoral thesis, she came across my story and reached out. Our conversations quickly revealed a shared purpose: understanding the lived experiences of those who stand up against powerful forces, and amplifying the voices of those who've endured the consequences of environmental neglect.

There are days when the weight of this work feels unbearable. When your own life and the lives of those you fight for seem too heavy to carry. When even the people you defend are indifferent or ungrateful. When the losses outnumber the wins—not defeats, because defeat is permanent, and we are not defeated. When loved ones suffer and die, and you begin to wonder if it's something in the air, the water, the land, or the soil.

It's in those quiet, lonely moments ... just you and God ... that a still, small voice asks, "If not you, then who will stand and fight?"

I'm not a religious zealot, but I am a person of faith. I believe a higher power guides our steps and equips us to overcome life's trials. In sharing that faith with Dr. Chavis, I found not only a kindred spirit but someone deeply committed to understanding the challenges faced by advocates like me and the communities we serve.

Rather than speak for others, I connected her with friends and neighbors willing to share their own stories. Because you can't talk about a life you haven't lived, their voices carry a truth and authenticity that no outsider can replicate.

Dr. Chavis's book is a powerful and elegant testament to those voices. It chronicles the lives of everyday people who have faced the devastating effects of climate change, pollution, and corporate greed. It presents the facts without sensationalism, honoring the dignity and resilience of those who continue to fight for justice in their communities.

I wholeheartedly endorse this book and encourage you to share it with friends, with book clubs, with anyone who believes in a greener, more equitable world. May its words inspire you, and may the stories within strengthen you on your own journey.

Above all, remember this world is still beautiful. We have the power to protect it. We only need to choose to let our light shine.

About the Author of the Foreword

John Beard Jr. is the founder and CEO of PACAN. After a thirty-eight-year career in the oil industry, he turned his focus to holding the industry accountable and became a leading community advocate in his hometown of Port Arthur, Texas. He founded PACAN to fight for health and safety protections in a region heavily impacted by refineries, export terminals, petrochemical plants, and the health consequences that come with them.

CONTENTS

Foreword	vii
Preface	1
Introduction	3
PART I: Environmental Racism and the Justice Movement	**9**
Chapter 1: The Color of Contamination	11
Chapter 2: Tracing Injustice: Through the Lens of Louisiana	23
Chapter 3: Structural Violence: How Environmental Racism Persists	35
PART II: Cases of Injustice	**45**
Chapter 4: Shingle Mountain	47
Chapter 5: The Flint Water Crisis	57
Chapter 6: Port Arthur's "Belly of the Beast"	67
Chapter 7: South Baltimore's Silent Killers	77
PART III: Activism, Resistance, and Resilience	**87**
Chapter 8: Progress Since the Landmark 1987 Study	89
Chapter 9: The Evolution of the EJ Movement	99
Chapter 10: Awareness to Action	109
Epilogue	125
Endnotes	129

PREFACE

In 2023, I completed my PhD in conflict analysis and resolution, building on my background in psychology and my interest in how people relate to and reconcile with one another. Early in the program, I enrolled in a course focused on conflicts that emerge within communities, particularly those rooted in race relations in the United States. To fulfill the course requirements, I was asked to analyze a race-based conflict, and I chose the Flint, Michigan, water crisis.

I had always been a student of Black history and an advocate for human rights; however, at the time of that course, I had not fully grasped the magnitude of environmental racism. Immersing myself in the Flint case proved transformative, and by the time I completed the case study, I was completely drawn in. I developed a deeper grasp of the systemic nature of environmental injustice while also examining how structural inequities and racialized policies shape the health and safety of entire communities.

What began as a class assignment became a personal and academic calling. I started researching other environmental injustice cases and was shocked to discover how many communities of color were living with the same pattern of neglect, exposure, and denial of harm. The more I researched, the more I learned; and the more I learned, the more I felt compelled to share that knowledge. Eventually, this passion led to my dissertation, "Unhealthy and Home: The Lived Experiences of African Americans Impacted by Environmental Racism in the United States." I have written this book to continue that work in an effort to honor the people who participated in my study and to fulfill my commitment to tell their stories. Each chapter reflects both their courage and the cycles of dispossession that continue to define the lived realities of so many communities.

My only frustration is that this book cannot give equal depth to every community affected by the same system of injustice. Indigenous peoples, Latinos, Asian Americans, Pacific Islanders, Middle Easterners, and immigrants from around the world all have borne environmental burdens shaped by race, class, and policy neglect. There is so much to this history—more than any single volume can contain.

My goal is not to provide a complete historical overview of this topic, but to open a door. I hope this book enlightens you and inspires you to continue learning about environmental justice and the many movements that sustain it. In Chapter 10, I include resources to help you begin or amplify your advocacy. My wish is that you will take what you learn here, share it with others, and join the growing chorus of voices fighting for what all people deserve: equal rights; healthy lives; and safe, clean neighborhoods.

INTRODUCTION

"I am sick and tired of being sick and tired, and we want a change."[1]

~ Fannie Lou Hamer (1917–1977)

Civil Rights Leader and Voting Rights Activist

Cofounder and Vice Chair of the
Mississippi Freedom Democratic Party;

Founder of the Freedom Farm Cooperative

ENVIRONMENTAL RACISM IS NOT a theoretical idea; it is a lived reality for millions of Americans. It is the quiet violence of toxic air, poisoned water, and neglected neighborhoods. It is the deliberate siting of hazardous facilities in communities of color, the disregard for environmental protections in poor neighborhoods, and the normalization of suffering among those least equipped to fight back.

Across the United States, both low-income communities and communities of color face disproportionate exposure to pollution, hazardous waste, and industrial risks.[2] They are more likely to live near refineries, landfills, and chemical plants; to breathe air laced with fine particulate matter; and to experience higher rates of asthma, cancer, and other pollution-related illnesses. These harms are compounded by policies that have long treated their neighborhoods as expendable in the name of economic growth.

The fact is that race is the greatest predictor of exposure to environmental toxins. This is not just a statistic; it is a lived experience for marginalized communities. African Americans, in particular, are 79% more likely than their White counterparts to live near dangerous industrial sites.[3] Their neighborhoods are often the chosen locations for hazardous facilities based on a long history of racialized land use and institutionalized discrimination.[4]

While this book is not a formal report of my research findings, it is deeply informed by a qualitative study I conducted with African American residents impacted by environmental racism. Their voices shape the narrative, offering insight into both personal trauma and collective resistance. I came to this work not just as a researcher, but as someone who has witnessed the toll of environmental injustice firsthand. This book is my way of honoring those stories and pushing for change.

To fully grasp the depth of their experiences, we must first define what environmental racism is and understand how it operates. "Environmental racism" refers to the disproportionate impact of environmental hazards on communities of color, often through deliberate policy decisions and systemic neglect. It is not an isolated injustice. It is woven into the larger tapestry of American inequality, stretching back to slavery, segregation, and the enduring myth of White superiority. It is a system that blames the oppressed for their oppression and then ignores their protests. It is the reason why residents of Flint, Michigan, were told to "just move," as if uprooting one's life were a simple solution to systemic harm.[5]

To understand how environmental racism persists, this book draws on the concept of "structural violence," which is the idea that social systems can inflict harm on marginalized groups through neglect, exclusion, and exploitation.[6] The consequences are not always visible, but they are deeply felt in the frustration of communities fighting to be heard.

I chose to focus on African American communities specifically because their experiences with environmental racism are among the most extensively documented and deeply rooted. This emphasis allows for a more nuanced exploration of how environmental injustice intersects with centuries of racial oppression and the policies that reproduce inequity. This is not meant to exclude other communities, but rather to illuminate a foundational pattern of injustice. The origins of environmental inequality in the U.S. are inseparable from the history of racial segregation. From Jim Crow–era zoning laws to redlining, African Americans were systematically confined to neighborhoods near industrial zones, floodplains, and other environmentally undesirable areas.[7] These patterns, reinforced through decades of discriminatory policy, ensured that Black communities were disproportionately exposed to hazard-emitting facilities.

Decades of research confirm that race, more than income, education, or geography, remains the strongest determinant of environmental exposure. The 1987 report *Toxic Wastes and Race in the United States*, published by the United Church of Christ's Commission for Racial Justice under the leadership of Rev. Dr. Benjamin F. Chavis Jr., found that communities of color were far more likely to live near hazardous waste sites than White Americans.[8] Subsequent studies by the Environmental

Protection Agency and leading universities have repeatedly reaffirmed this finding, illustrating that these disparities are not accidental but structural.[9]

The modern environmental justice movement itself was born out of African American activism. The 1982 protests in Warren County, North Carolina, where Black residents were arrested for opposing the siting of a polychlorinated biphenyl (PCB) landfill in their community, marked a pivotal moment in linking environmental health to civil rights.[10] Scholars and advocates such as Dr. Robert D. Bullard, Dr. Beverly Wright, and Dr. Benjamin Chavis built upon that foundation, revealing how environmental harm reflects the same systems of inequality that have long governed access to housing, healthcare, and political representation.[11]

Geography is inextricably tied to these inequities. Many historically Black communities are situated in industrial corridors across the South—from Louisiana's Cancer Alley to Houston's Manchester neighborhood to Port Arthur, Texas—where economic segregation and racial discrimination converge to create what Dr. Wright calls "the geography of risk."[12] These landscapes illustrate how systemic racism becomes spatial, embedding inequality into the physical environment.

Centering the Black experience therefore provides a crucial foundation for understanding environmental injustice more broadly. African American communities were among the first to document and resist these inequities, creating the frameworks of advocacy, law, and scholarship that continue to guide environmental justice movements today. Focusing on their struggle clarifies, rather than narrows, the lens of structural environmental harm.

At the same time, it's essential to recognize that environmental racism extends beyond any one community. Latino, Indigenous, and other populations across the United States continue to suffer from disproportionate exposure to pollution, unsafe housing conditions, and the effects of climate change and infrastructure neglect. Their stories are equally vital to understanding the full scope of this crisis. While this book centers on African American voices, it stands in solidarity with all communities fighting for their ecological freedom.

Whether you are new to this topic, a policymaker, a community organizer, an environmental advocate, or someone seeking to understand how race and place intersect in America, this book is for you. In the chapters that follow, you will trace the origins and evolution of environmental racism, beginning with the birth of the justice movement and the historical roots of racial oppression in America. You will explore how systemic racism manifests through structural violence and examine four powerful case studies: Shingle Mountain, the Flint water crisis, Port Arthur's industrial concentration, and South Baltimore's industrial incinerators. Later chapters reflect on the progress made since the landmark 1987 study, the growth of the environmental justice movement, and practical ways readers can engage in advocacy and drive change in their own communities. What follows is not just an academic account: It is a call to action, a demand for accountability, and a tribute to those who continue to fight for the dignity of their communities.

PART I

Environmental Racism and the Justice Movement

"The beauty of anti-racism is that you don't have to pretend to be free of racism to be anti-racist. Anti-racism is the commitment to fight racism wherever you find it, including in yourself. And it's the only way forward."[13]

~ **Ijeoma Oluo**

Writer, Speaker, Social Critic

Author of *So You Want to Talk About Race*; *Mediocre: The Dangerous Legacy of White Male America*; and *Be a Revolution: How Everyday People Are Fighting Oppression and Changing the World—and How You Can, Too*

CHAPTER ONE

The Color of Contamination

"Regardless of the city, it's the same issue and it's the same people."[14]

~ **Dr. Robert D. Bullard**

The Father of Environmental Justice

Distinguished Professor of Urban Planning and Environmental Policy and Founding Director of the Bullard Center for Environmental and Climate Justice at Texas Southern University

NEARLY TWENTY YEARS BEFORE the emergence of the environmental justice (EJ) movement, the Reverend Dr. Martin Luther King Jr. stood on the steps of the Lincoln Memorial before an estimated crowd of 250,000 and delivered his soul-stirring "I Have a Dream" speech.[15] Dr. King predicted that the journey toward freedom and equality would be long and arduous, yet his speech was permeated with hope for a country where all people, regardless of race or religion, would one day be united. Dr. King's speech had a resounding impact on our nation; it was inarguably one of the most powerful orations in the discourse on civil rights. He maintained that freedom and racial equality were at the heart of the social justice movement, a struggle that ultimately cost him his life. Lamentably, six decades after the March on Washington, Dr. King's dream of equal rights remains unfulfilled.

The civil rights movement was born out of a need to eradicate systemic racial injustices that disadvantaged African American people and their neighborhoods. Early pioneers for civil rights demanded equal treatment for all minorities, a subset of the American population who found themselves disenfranchised in nearly all aspects of everyday life. Notwithstanding their core demands—the end of racial segregation and race-based violence, the pursuit of economic justice, and the protection of voting rights—the need for equal housing, neighborhood investment, and environmental protection began to give rise to separate yet parallel issues for the movement.[16]

Initially, the push to address housing inequities and environmental harm was folded into the broader civil rights agenda, but it often became overshadowed by other urgent battles for equality. By the late 1970s, the campaign for environmental justice became a movement of its own, with grassroots organizers aiming to confront and resist the disproportionate siting of hazardous facilities in communities of color. This pattern persists well into the twenty-first century.[17]

Environmental racism is so embedded in American social systems that it negatively affects generations of individuals and groups based on race, while providing and maintaining privilege for the more dominant group.[18] This type of systemic racism puts undue burdens on communities of color, resulting in "sacrifice zones," which are almost always in majority-minority neighborhoods where the land is viewed as expendable.[19] These patterns of harm exemplify what scholars such as Johan

Galtung have called "structural violence," the systemic ways in which institutions and policies, though seemingly neutral, inflict harm on marginalized groups by denying them access to safety, good health, and economic opportunity. Within this framework, environmental racism can be understood not as isolated acts of discrimination but as the cumulative outcome of political and economic structures designed to prioritize some lives over others.[20] These dynamics are not confined to theory; they determine the lived conditions in countless towns and cities nationwide.

Take, for instance, the more than four decades of pollution that have contaminated the waterways and unlined landfills in Anniston, Alabama, whose predominately Black residents "had the highest recorded levels of PCBs [polychlorinated biphenyls] in the nation" after the Monsanto Company dumped thousands of pounds of the toxic chemical around their homes and into their local water supply.[21] Or consider the 85-mile stretch of historically Black-populated towns in Louisiana, now dubbed "Cancer Alley," where generations of families settled along the Mississippi River following the Civil War.[22] That region is called Cancer Alley due to residents' disturbingly high cancer rates, which are linked to the area's industrial growth and expansion.[23] For the people living in these toxic communities, prolonged chemical exposure to environmental hazards leads to grave health repercussions, a diminished quality of life, and a shortened life span.[24]

Dr. Robert Bullard, widely known as the father of environmental justice, is a leading advocate of the EJ movement, supporting the elimination and prevention of unjust and inequitable environmental conditions. As a prominent leader of the movement, he has helped to define "environmental racism" and has given voice to millions of Americans directly affected by the targeted, discriminatory practice of siting toxic waste facilities in their neighborhoods. He has also provided a critical lens through which to understand the lethal environmental injustices that harm those who are living in these areas when bad actors, including zoning boards and corporations, act with callous disregard for human life.

According to Dr. Bullard, environmental racism is any policy or practice that disadvantages any individual or group because of their race.[25] Furthermore, it is "the disproportionate exposure of underprivileged racial and ethnic groups to environmental disease factors,"[26] as well as the exclusion of people of color from policymaking boards (both public and private), commissions, regulatory bodies, and environmental nonprofit organizations.[27] It is, as Robert W. Collin defined it, "race-based differential enforcement of environmental rules and regulations."[28] These definitions have anchored legal battles that exposed the very injustices Bullard referenced.

Bean v. Southwestern Waste Management Corp. (1979) was a landmark environmental racism case that catalyzed the EJ movement because it was the first of its kind to be adjudicated as a civil rights case. The plaintiff, a Houston resident named Margaret Bean living in a predominantly Black neighborhood, was represented by attorney Linda McKeever Bullard. McKeever Bullard, wife of Robert Bullard, made the case for racial discrimination in the construction of a municipal landfill in Bean's neighborhood.

McKeever Bullard argued before the judge, albeit unsuccessfully, that there was a violation of Title VI of the 1964 Civil Rights Act (Section 601), which states, "No person in the United States shall, on the ground of race, color, or national origin, be excluded from participation in, be denied the benefits of, or be subjected to discrimination under any program or activity receiving Federal financial assistance."[29] Because the Texas Department of Health (TDH) was a state agency that participated in federally funded programs, its actions were subject to the antidiscrimination protections offered under Title VI. McKeever Bullard's legal strategy contended that TDH's approval in granting the Southwestern Waste Management Corporation a permit to site the waste facility in Margaret Bean's neighborhood was evidence of discrimination.

At the urging of his wife, Dr. Robert Bullard, a trained sociologist and then–assistant professor at Texas Southern University, initiated a statistical study in which he and his students compiled local data from the prior five decades (the 1930s through 1978) to determine the placement of every landfill and incinerator in the Houston area. The most revelatory finding from the study that convinced McKeever Bullard to pursue the case as a civil rights matter was a pattern, she would argue, of racial discrimination that resulted in more than 80% of the facilities being placed in Black neighborhoods, despite Houston's racial makeup being only 25% African American at the time of the study.[30]

Although the evidence was damning, the court ruled against the plaintiffs because proving racial *intent* to discriminate is notoriously difficult. Circumstantial evidence may reflect an undeniable pattern, but it often falls short of the high standard of compelling proof. Nonetheless, this data was later added to the canon of EJ literature, and Dr. Bullard launched a movement with his classic work *Dumping in Dixie: Race, Class, and Environmental Quality*.[31]

Another lawsuit, *Warren County v. State of North Carolina* (1981), alleged racial discrimination in the siting of a PCB landfill in Afton, North Carolina. As in Houston several years earlier, this suit was litigated as a civil rights case under the same legal basis—that there was a federal Title VI violation of the Civil Rights Act of 1964: Warren County was targeted because of its racial makeup. Nonetheless, Federal District Judge W. Earl Britt was quick to refute the basis for the suit by emphatically stating, "There is not one shred of evidence that race has at any time been a motivating factor for any decision taken by any official—state, federal, or local."[32] When Afton residents took to the streets with signs, chants, and songs hearkening back to the civil rights protests of the sixties, it was considered by some a last resort to save their neighborhood.

Afton is remembered by historians as the birthplace of the EJ movement. It wasn't the first time that a group of minorities mobilized to voice their grievances over the unwanted use of land. However, it was the first time that a community of color, made up of those without political clout, was on the national stage challenging their community's selection as the site for a toxic dumping ground.[33] The residents, 60%–80% of whom identified as African American, protested; some placed their bodies before steel trucks to form a human blockade in an attempt to disrupt the state-sanctioned dumping of nearly 3,200 truckloads of highly toxic soil. The soil was laced with carcinogenic PCBs and was to be deposited at the newly constructed landfill in their neighborhood, which was built primarily to contain the contaminated soil collected from the brazen act of industrial abuse perpetrated when the Ward Transformer Company of Raleigh illegally dumped over 30,000 gallons of contaminated oil across hundreds of miles of North Carolina's landscape.[34]

While residents fought to protect their community, the Environmental Protection Agency (EPA), the regulatory body established in 1970 and authorized by Congress to enforce environmental laws, was supposed to be fulfilling its mission of benefiting and protecting *all* citizens, regardless of race or class, from environmental hazards affecting them.[35] Despite this mission, and acting in less than good faith, the EPA waived the protections that would have provided more stringent regulatory oversight of the construction of the Warren County PCB landfill.[36] While granting the waivers was legally permissible, the landfill failed to meet the expected standard for the prevention of dire health risks: Its shallow water table—just seven feet below the surface—put groundwater at risk from PCB leaching, which would make it unsafe to drink.[37]

Following months of mounting local resistance, the grassroots protests escalated to a tipping point on September 15, 1982, with the arrival of the first truck. Protests ensued for over six weeks, through mid-October 1982, resulting in approximately five hundred arrests, with some protesters resisting by having their bodies go limp as they were carted off to jail.[38]

The Afton residents who had aligned themselves with neighboring organizations, including the local chapter of the National Association for the Advancement of Colored People (NAACP), did not succeed in stopping the state from dumping PCBs in Afton, but their persistence captured the attention of the nation. It raised awareness of the need for environmental oversight and spotlighted other regions subjected to similar abuse. The protests became a catalyst for legal, scientific, and policy reform, setting the stage for what would become the four defining pillars of the modern EJ movement: courtroom challenge, grassroots mobilization, empirical research, and federal recognition.[39]

Walter Fauntroy, a pastor and delegate to the House of Representatives (who also chaired the Congressional Black Caucus in 1983), was present at the Afton protests and was arrested while demonstrating. Upon his return to Washington, D.C., he set into motion a nonpartisan, independent study by the U.S. General Accounting Office (GAO), which was commissioned in response to the protests. The regional study focused on four hazardous waste landfills in the states of Alabama, South Carolina, and North Carolina. It found that 75%, or three out of the four landfills, were placed in communities of color, with race being a greater predictor than income for their placement.[40]

A subsequent landmark study in 1987 titled *Toxic Wastes and Race in the United States: A National Report on the Racial and Socio-Economic Characteristics of Communities with Hazardous Waste Sites* offered powerful insights into a national pattern of environmental injustice across the country by looking at the racial and socioeconomic characteristics of communities near 413 commercially operating hazardous waste facilities in the U.S. as of May 1986.[41] One part of the study used population data, derived from the 1980 census, of over 36,000 residential zip codes to analyze the racial composition of communities in and around over 18,000 uncontrolled toxic waste sites, as defined by the study.[42] According to the report, "uncontrolled toxic waste sites refer to closed and abandoned sites on the EPA's list of sites which pose a present and potential threat to human health and the environment."[43] Spearheaded by Dr. Benjamin Chavis, then–executive director of the United Church of Christ Commission for Racial Justice (UCC-CRJ), and researcher Charles Lee, then-director of the UCC-CRJ's Special Project on Toxic Injustice, the study underscored race as the single-most important factor in the location of commercial hazardous waste facilities, among the variables tested.[44] Dr. Bullard later affirmed the UCC report's findings, noting that "the study found that race was the most powerful explanatory factor for where toxic facilities were located across the country. It was not income; it was not property values; it was not whether people owned or rented; it was not land values. It was *race.*"[45]

White people, who historically have a greater percentage of homeownership and more economic power than Black people, can often influence the placement of these facilities.[46] With the NIMBY ("Not in My Backyard") movement, developers and other bad actors gravitate toward minoritized neighborhoods where residents are often economically depressed and have limited political power.[47] These residents are often perceived as putting up little to no resistance when locally unwanted land uses (LULUs), including landfills and processing plants, are placed near their homes.[48]

Based on research from 2008 by Downey and Hawkins, African American households with incomes between $50,000 and $60,000 live in neighborhoods that are more polluted than neighborhoods in which White households with incomes below $10,000 live,[49] making the corroborating point that it's easier for a low-income White family to move into a less environmentally toxic neighborhood than for a Black family to do the same. According to Dr. Bullard, "even middle-class African American neighborhoods sometimes lack basic utilities and adequate sanitary services."[50] Income levels alone do not protect Blacks from exposure to polluted neighborhoods. "For example, to this day, majority-White and wealthy communities are where investments into infrastructure are more likely to be made, where environmental laws are more likely to be properly enforced, and where polluters are more likely to be held accountable or kept away entirely."[51]

Potentially, some are betting against people of color in sacrifice zones, banking on their possessing lower resistance and less personal agency to respond to unilateral, nonconsensual decisions that negatively affect them the most.[52] Lack of minority representation on county boards and other policymaking panels only perpetuates environmentally racist practices. These types of structural barriers make participatory engagement more challenging and act as a systemic deterrent to achieving the necessary representation for profound change.[53]

Recognizing the mounting evidence that communities of color are disproportionately exposed to environmental pollutants from hazardous waste facilities and other contamination sources, the EPA established the Office of Environmental Justice in 1992.[54] The office was created to ensure that the agency's policies and programs were implemented in an environmentally just manner, reflecting a growing awareness that race and class were significant predictors of exposure to environmental harm. Despite this institutional step, the persistence of inequities across vulnerable communities revealed that policy creation alone was insufficient without enforcement and accountability.[55]

Dismally, over two decades later, in 2016, a U.S. Commission on Civil Rights report found that the EPA repeatedly failed to provide prompt and meaningful support to communities of color unless external pressure demanded it.[56] In addition, there is evidence to suggest some corporate polluters intentionally disregard EPA regulations, with little challenge, due to lax public policies, limited agency funding and staffing, and the EPA's inability to monitor the remediation of every violation.[57] This perpetual cycle of neglect keeps disenfranchised communities at greater risk for environmental harm, a practice that has historical roots stretching as far back as Reconstruction.[58]

Though the EPA's record has fallen short, the persistence of affected communities continues to challenge complacency. Each protest, study, and lawsuit has contributed to an expanding body of knowledge and a moral urgency that propels the movement forward. The environmental justice struggle is, at its core, a testament to the resilience of ordinary people who refuse to accept that pollution, neglect, and inequality are inevitable. Across the nation, new generations of advocates, scientists, and residents continue to build on this foundation. Using digital tools, data transparency, and community-based research, they reaffirm a simple truth first voiced on the streets of Afton: the belief that every community, regardless of race or class, deserves the right to breathe clean air, drink safe water, and live free from harm.[59]

CHAPTER TWO

Tracing Injustice: Through the Lens of Louisiana

"We can decide in this moment as Americans: Are we going to enter another nadir, or are we going to push back against that and continue to pursue an egalitarian society? This is an inflection point, and I fear that because we don't understand that history, we don't know that you can gain rights in the United States and you can lose those rights almost completely."[60]

~ **Nikole Hannah-Jones**

Pulitzer Prize–Winning Journalist

Creator of The 1619 Project; Knight Chair in Race and Journalism at Howard University

THERE'S AN 85-MILE STRETCH of land along the Mississippi River in Louisiana known as "Cancer Alley," where history and industry converge to reveal the enduring link between race, place, and environmental injustice.[61] With over 150 petrochemical plants and oil refineries, as well as other densely concentrated industrial facilities, it is a major hub of the United States petrochemical industry.[62] While exact production percentages vary, the region is essential to both the national economy and global markets.[63] Its emergence as a petrochemical hub began in the

1940s and 1950s, when companies sought to locate numerous refineries in the River Parishes along the Mississippi River for their proximity to shipping routes, which provided easy access for transport.[64] Although it created jobs, the industrial growth also generated extensive pollution that has resulted in severe health outcomes for those living in and around this corridor.[65]

Residents of Cancer Alley have some of the highest rates of cancer in the country, as well as co-occurring illnesses, which pose constant challenges for families who live in the shadow of industrial facilities.[66] By the 1980s, the public health crisis tied to this part of the Gulf South had become undeniable.[67] Reports of cancer fatalities, widespread cases of chronic and childhood asthma, and high rates of miscarriage revealed the heavy toll of industrial pollution on residents' quality of life.[68] Cancer Alley reflected a national pattern in which profit was placed above public health and became a stark microcosm illustrating the devastating effects of environmental racism.[69] It is a place where economic growth and corporate expansion were prioritized while the health and safety of the most disadvantaged communities were sacrificed.[70] To understand how this region became so heavily burdened, we must look beyond the smokestacks and pipelines to the social and historical foundations that made such exploitation possible. The story of Cancer Alley did not begin with modern industry; it began generations earlier, when the promise of emancipation collided with systems built to preserve racial hierarchy.[71]

The Thirteenth, Fourteenth, and Fifteenth Amendments to the United States Constitution—known as the Reconstruction Amendments because they were ratified after the Civil War in

1865—abolished slavery, granted citizenship to all those naturalized or born in the U.S., provided equal protection under the law, and gave Black men the right to vote.[72] These amendments marked a monumental shift in American society, though White supremacist systems quickly mobilized to undermine them. It's during this period of history that Black Louisianans, most of whom were newly freed, had the opportunity to acquire small plots of land and begin farming independently. Many families settled on the rural acres of former sugarcane and cotton plantations along the river, seeking stability and community.[73]

Their efforts to cultivate and own land were soon obstructed with state laws like the Black Codes (1865 to 1867), which prohibited Black people from owning real estate or land outright.[74] Designed by White lawmakers, these codes curtailed the newfound freedom of the formerly enslaved and ensured African Americans remained trapped in a system that closely mirrored slavery.[75] By denying them the ability to own property legally, the state prevented freedmen and their families from building economic independence or creating stable homesteads. The restrictions guaranteed that Black Louisianans remained subordinate to the political and economic dominance of White planters, effectively nullifying many of the rights supposedly secured by emancipation.[76]

The most punitive measures within the Black Codes were the vagrancy and apprenticeship laws, intended to maintain Black labor dependency through criminalization.[77] Vagrancy laws rendered unemployment illegal for freed people, regardless of circumstance or lack of opportunity. Those who were thought to be "idle" were fined or arrested for loitering, punished simply for existing outside the plantation economy.

While incarcerated, a system of "convict leasing" allowed state governments to lease their prisoners to plantations, railroads, and other private enterprises, effectively creating a pipeline of forced labor that overwhelmingly targeted Black men.[78] Convict leasing generated state revenue while simultaneously restoring the no-wage labor pool that had been lost with emancipation. When state governments were faced with financial strain, incarceration rates for African Americans rose sharply, ensuring a steady supply of labor and re-entrenching the community in forced servitude. The inhumane treatment of those imprisoned resulted in high mortality rates, reflecting conditions that perpetuated slavery's brutality within the criminal justice system.[79]

Children were also ensnared by the Black Codes. Apprenticeship laws bound emancipated children, some as young as three, to White "sponsors," often their families' former enslavers.[80] These arrangements removed children from their homes and deprived families of parental authority. Involuntary apprenticeships denied education and guaranteed continued economic exploitation, ensuring literacy and mobility remained out of reach. Such mechanisms were calculated efforts to reassert racial hierarchy under a legal facade, undermining the possibility of genuine freedom for future generations of African Americans.[81]

Although the Black Codes restricted ownership, federal policies like the Southern Homestead Act of 1866 offered a narrow path to land acquisition.[82] The lands were often marginal and difficult to farm, but freed families persisted. African Americans demonstrated determination, acquiring modest holdings despite immense social and financial pressure. Many of the tracts were considered undesirable due to poor soil, flood risk, or distance from markets, but freed people valued them as a foundation for self-sufficiency. Despite constant obstacles, African American families worked their land and passed it to their descendants.

Intergenerational property ownership gave families and communities continuity and resilience, helping them withstand the systemic efforts that sought to dispossess them. As a case in point, Black multigenerational land ownership, intertwined with a rich cultural heritage, made the Mississippi River region a vital tributary of Black life. These communities, built out of hardship, established strong networks centered on family, church, and agriculture. Residents in these historically African American towns developed and continued to maintain deep ties to the land, valuing it as both livelihood and legacy.

The withdrawal of federal troops from the South in 1877 signaled the end of Reconstruction and the erosion of federally enforced protections.[83] Without federal oversight, White supremacist groups and local governments reasserted control, dismantling the limited progress African Americans had achieved. The demise of Reconstruction paved the way for a new wave of oppression—the Jim Crow era.[84] Spanning the late nineteenth through mid-twentieth centuries, Jim Crow laws enforced racial segregation and suppressed Black political and economic power. Segregation penetrated schools, transportation, and public facilities, while violence and intimidation reinforced its grip.[85] These laws encroached on every aspect of African American life, including landownership, access to resources, and legal recourse.[86] Local courts routinely refused to honor property deeds or contracts, stripping African Americans of economic security. This systematic denial ensured that power, wealth, and land remained consolidated in White hands.[87] The inequalities embedded during this period laid the groundwork for the next phase of exploitation, when post-war industrialization would follow the racial boundaries established by Jim Crow.

During the post–World War II industrial boom, chemical plants and oil refineries clustered around rural and semirural sacrifice zones and fence-line communities where economically disadvantaged African Americans were concentrated. Industrial developers targeted these locations because the land was cheap and political resistance was minimal. Urban centers were not spared either. Predominantly Black cities such as Detroit and Baltimore had already become industrial hubs, where segregation laws and restrictive covenants confined minorities to racially designated districts. These legal practices ensured that minorities remained in neighborhoods most exposed to environmental and social stressors while being denied access to safer, better-resourced areas.

From the early 1950s through the 1970s, another powerful demographic shift occurred as White Americans fled cities for segregated suburbs, a migration known as "White flight."[88] This movement deepened urban segregation and hollowed out the tax bases of many metropolitan areas. White suburban enclaves enjoyed stronger political representation and greater capacity to resist industrial siting, while those left behind—primarily people of color—lacked comparable power. African Americans, regardless of income or education, faced discriminatory practices that excluded them from White suburban neighborhoods and trapped them in urban zones increasingly burdened by pollution and poverty.

Professor David R. Williams of the Harvard T.H. Chan School of Public Health posits that "one of America's best-kept secrets is how residential segregation is the secret source that creates inequality in the United States."[89] Dr. Williams is one of the most influential voices in public health and social science.[90] His scholarship has shown how segregation not only relates to physical boundaries but reinforces inequalities across racial lines.[91] His references to "hypersegregation" explain the concentrated disadvantages in minoritized communities that create multidimensional disparities.[92] In essence, hypersegregation not only separates populations but also magnifies inequities through the intersection of social challenges related to housing, healthcare, education, and employment.[93]

Champions of the civil rights movement sought to dismantle the structural barriers created by segregation and discrimination. As Nikole Hannah-Jones of The 1619 Project notes, the passage of the Civil Rights Act of 1964, the Voting Rights Act of 1965, and the Fair Housing Act of 1968 were hard-won victories for African Americans still struggling to secure constitutional rights supposedly guaranteed a century earlier.[94] These landmark statutes outlawed segregation, prohibited racial discrimination in voting, and expanded equal access to housing.[95] They became law only after decades of organizing, sustained protest, and legal battles that demanded the Constitution's promises be honored in practice. However, even as the civil rights movement achieved monumental legal victories, new forms of exclusion took hold.[96] Economic and spatial policies determined where people could live, what resources they could access, and how environmental burdens were distributed. Chief among these was redlining.

Beginning in the 1930s, the Home Owners' Loan Corporation (HOLC) produced "residential security maps" that graded neighborhoods from A to D. Affluent, predominantly White areas typically received A ratings, while Black or racially mixed neighborhoods were often graded D and outlined in red, hence the term "redlining."[97] Banks and federal lenders used these maps to deny loans and mortgages in redlined areas, locking African Americans out of affordable credit and homeownership. Financial decisions were based not on an applicant's reliability but on neighborhood racial composition.[98] As a result, property values stagnated, municipal services deteriorated, and families were forced into exploitative land contracts with no protections. Though illegal today, redlining's aftereffects still prevail.[99] Homes once redlined have appreciated far less in value, producing a racial wealth gap that constrains education, entrepreneurship, and intergenerational inheritance. Even after the Fair Housing Act outlawed the practice, predatory lending and systematic undervaluation continued to suppress wealth accumulation in majority-minority neighborhoods.[100]

Dr. Robert Bullard's research directly links the legacy of redlining to the siting of modern sacrifice zones. Bullard argues that discriminatory zoning and siting policies are "compatible with pollution," producing what he calls "outdoor apartheid."[101] Environmental racism, in this sense, enforces a de facto segregation in which hazardous industries are systematically placed near marginalized communities.[102] He also notes that homeowners in formerly redlined areas face greater difficulty securing insurance or disaster assistance, a disparity laid bare by events such as Hurricanes Katrina and Harvey. In these crises, historical devaluation translated into delayed or insufficient aid, which magnified the racial and economic inequities embedded in disaster response systems.[103]

A 2018 study by researchers from Rice University and the University of Pittsburgh found that as Federal Emergency Management Agency (FEMA) assistance increased across U.S. communities, racial and economic wealth inequality also increased.[104] Wealthier White households gained in net worth following natural disasters, while Blacks (and Hispanics), on average, saw losses, even when communities experienced comparable levels of physical damage.[105]

The Rice–Pittsburgh longitudinal study tracked 3,500 families from 1999 to 2013 and accounted for FEMA aid received, physical damages for the respective natural disaster, and demographics.[106] Over the course of the study period, the wealth of affluent White households increased by an average of $126,000, whereas African American households lost $27,000 on average due to unequal access to disaster aid and insurance.[107] Disaster recovery funds are frequently tied to property values. However, because historical practices like redlining deliberately devalued African American neighborhoods, property appraisals in these areas are often unfairly low, leading to inequitable allocations of recovery assistance.[108]

Amid these persistent inequities, federal policymakers began to acknowledge that environmental harms were not evenly shared, and recognition of such inequities eventually shaped federal environmental policy. In 1994, President Bill Clinton issued Executive Order 12898 on environmental justice, directing federal agencies to ensure that minority and low-income populations were not disproportionately affected by environmental hazards.[109] This order provided a framework for integrating equity into federal decision-making, pressing agencies such as FEMA to consider justice in disaster management.[110] Yet meaningful implementation depended on state and local commitment, and because local zoning controls often overrode or weakened federal guidance, enforcement remained uneven, allowing pollution burdens to persist in marginalized communities.

Discriminatory zoning has harmed both rural and urban areas. In rural Louisiana, Black farmers and landowners were frequently assigned unfavorable zoning classifications that depressed property values and curtailed development.[111] In urban centers, neglect in city planning and infrastructure investment caused physical and social decline in minority neighborhoods.[112] Whether in countryside or city, both groups have been systematically excluded from resources and political influence, reinforcing cycles of deprivation.[113]

Even in urban slums, historically privileged groups have been suspected of deliberately alienating African Americans and other minorities from policymaking boards.[114] Researchers in the EJ field have long suggested that this exclusion from decision-making panels is not an accident but an intentional strategy of disempowerment designed to silence voices most affected by environmental decisions.[115] Since at least the early 1990s, researchers have exposed state and local agencies for exclusionary practices such as cherry-picking board members who supported industrial and political interests rather than community advocates who are impartial or stand in opposition to those industries.[116] Public meetings were frequently scheduled in locations that were inaccessible by public transportation or held at inconvenient hours, limiting working-class participation.[117] Additionally, some local officials imposed English-only policies in predominantly non-English-speaking communities, shutting out grassroots leaders and dismissing testimonies, which further excluded vulnerable groups from the decision-making process.[118] When zoning boards, established by local governing bodies, designate specific neighborhoods for industrial use, they effectively roll out the red carpet for corporations to build their facilities regardless of the residents' concerns.[119] This recurring pattern, from exclusionary zoning to token participation, reveals how environmental injustice is sustained not only by pollutants in the air, but also by policies that silence those most affected.[120]

The industrial landscapes encircling Cancer Alley reveal how injustice operates as a form of structural violence. This violence is sustained by zoning laws and political indifference, which normalize harm in plain sight.[121] Over generations, public health and community vitality have been quietly exchanged for industrial profit, leaving residents to bear the cumulative burden of contamination and neglect.[122] Cancer Alley exemplifies how discrimination and economic interest converge to endanger American lives under the guise of progress. It is an ever-present reminder that the same lands once used for human exploitation now bear the weight of modern industry, demonstrating how geography and policy can work in tandem to disadvantage those with the least power to resist. Recognizing these historical continuities is essential to understanding how structural racism continues to shape access to safe, livable environments. Achieving genuine equity and protection will require the nation to fundamentally reimagine its land-use priorities and the values guiding public policy itself.[123]

CHAPTER THREE

Structural Violence: How Environmental Racism Persists

"The violence is built into the structure and shows up as unequal power and consequently as unequal life chances."[124]

~ **Johan Galtung (1930–2024)**

Pioneer of Peace and Conflict Studies

Founder of the Peace Research Institute Oslo (PRIO); Distinguished Professor of Peace Studies

JOHAN GALTUNG, A NORWEGIAN sociologist and a pioneering figure in peace and conflict studies, was the first scholar to introduce the groundbreaking theoretical framework of structural violence. His influential 1969 article titled "Violence, Peace, and Peace Research" marked a critical turning point in the field of peace studies, as it expanded the scope of how violence is understood, shifting focus away from solely physical acts of aggression toward more subtle—yet equally destructive—institutional neglect. His work laid the foundation for comprehending violence as a broader condition embedded in social systems.

Galtung conceptualized structural violence as any social structure or institution that systematically prevents an individual or group from reaching their fullest potential in life.[125] This theoretical framework underscores the idea that violence is not restricted to overt acts like war or assault, but it instead exists in routine functioning and norms that harm marginalized groups. Moreover, structural violence encompasses conditions such as poverty and subordination that result in the denial of access to essential resources and opportunities for advancement.[126] In effect, Galtung sought to expose the barriers that deny human beings the chance to fulfill their basic material, physiological, and psychological needs.

Structural violence is both pervasive and insidious because it blurs the boundaries between intention and consequence. The harm it produces is often not the outcome of deliberate acts, but rather it emerges from the routine operations of unequal systems.[127] For instance, a city may justify placing an industrial facility near a low-income neighborhood as an economic necessity. Yet the long-term health consequences for residents expose a form of violence woven into policy and practice. When such decisions consistently affect low-income populations or communities of color, the violence becomes structural, a predictable outcome of a stratified social order.

Contemporary scholars argue that structural violence is shaped not only by abstract systems, but also by individual behaviors and beliefs that maintain it over time.[128] This continuity exists because people and their practices play a critical role in how violence becomes naturalized. It is enacted and sustained through the choices of policymakers, corporate leaders, regulators, and even everyday citizens who uphold widely accepted cultural norms.

These theorists also emphasize that structural violence operates beneath the surface of daily life, often eluding detection. Environmental racism, for example, may not be immediately recognized as violent, yet prolonged exposure to hazardous pollutants can inflict deep and enduring harm. Because these injuries accumulate gradually, they rarely trigger the kind of public outrage associated with more overt forms of aggression, making them harder to recognize and remedy.

Examining EJ through the critical lens of Galtung's framework helps explain how environmental racism persists and who benefits from its continuation. It also highlights how structural inequities are ingrained in the way political, economic, and social institutions are organized,[129] inflicting harm on individuals and groups, and constituting a pernicious form of violence that is profoundly damaging. It is more than just failed policies or corporate negligence, but instead a larger system where racial and economic hierarchies determine who is protected and who is left vulnerable. It is in this vein that the intrusion of locally unwanted land uses (LULUs) in or around communities of color has become a pattern of placing hazard-emitting facilities in areas deemed "less valuable," reflecting deliberate and historically held discriminatory practices.

It is worth noting that violence in this sense is not only caused by the siting of hazard-emitting facilities, but by how laws are applied differently. Researchers have found stronger enforcement and stricter regulatory oversight in predominantly White neighborhoods, often attributed to their effective exertion of political strength and advocacy. Yet this disparity also reflects structural biases in governmental responsiveness, resulting in unequal protection across racial and socioeconomic lines. Environmental agencies typically respond more quickly, impose harsher penalties, and maintain higher inspection rates when complaints arise from affluent or predominantly White areas.[130] In contrast, communities of color frequently experience lax enforcement, regulatory neglect, and disregard by environmental agencies or local authorities.[131] This is largely due to the perception that there will be very little resistance or opposition from communities whose grievances have been historically suppressed.[132] Structural oppression of this kind is a manifestation of how power and privilege dictate whose voices matter, whose health is prioritized, and whose safety is considered expendable.

Prominent conflict resolution scholar Dennis J. D. Sandole espouses the view that structural violence is typically directed toward minority groups whose access to crucial resources is systematically denied, largely because of who they are rather than anything they have done.[133] This dynamic is especially evident in environmental contexts, where individuals and communities experience disproportionate exposure to polluted air, unsafe drinking water, and degraded living conditions as a direct result of their social position within an already unequal system. This premise forms the bedrock of normalized racial exclusion, with officially sanctioned regulatory decisions that target underrepresented populations.

African Americans, in particular, have endured a legacy of institutionalized oppression that has shaped the realities of their housing, land use, education, healthcare, and employment. The cumulative effects of such have perpetuated cycles of disadvantage, codifying inequality into law and practice in ways that often appear "neutral" on the surface while producing extremely unfavorable outcomes. As a result, decisions that are directly counter to their best interests are often made unilaterally by powerful industry players or government agencies.

While Galtung's theory provides a conceptual lens for understanding how social systems inflict harm, critical race theory offers a complementary framework for explaining why certain populations disproportionately bear that harm. According to Derrick Bell, inequality exists because the systems in the United States are intentionally designed to maintain and legitimize the status quo.[134] This is the basis for why racism is difficult to challenge, as those in the dominant social group seek to protect and preserve their existing power structure.[135] He contended that racism is not a temporary failure of the American system but a permanent and integral feature of it, designed to maintain the privileges of the dominant group.[136] Furthermore, Bell's theory of racial realism argues that anti-Black sentiments are a permanent problem, and that despite protests and legal reform, racism will persevere.[137] While Bell asserts that protesting racism is morally obligatory, racism is resilient and adaptive, capable of reshaping itself to fit new social and legal contexts.[138]

Bell's critical race theory and Galtung's structural violence theory intersect in their recognition that systemic inequalities are embedded within social institutions. Environmental racism exemplifies this intersection and can be understood as an "inherited" form of structural violence;[139] that is, it is reproduced across generations and increasingly accepted as inevitable. This broad acceptance occurs among those who are directly impacted as well as society at large.

Within this broader system, minorities are routinely blamed for the oppressive conditions they face, and their legitimate protests and demands for justice are frequently dismissed by those entrusted with their protection.[140] This dismissal takes many forms, from minimizing community concerns during public hearings to ignoring scientific data that highlights disparate impacts. This callous conduct only fuels distrust between the disadvantaged groups and relevant institutions, hampering efforts to create healthy living arrangements.

The long-held belief that African Americans are not interested in their environmental conditions could not be further from the truth. The EJ movement was birthed in rebellion to such a threat. Nevertheless, public officials continue to reinforce a false narrative that erases the legitimacy of residents' lived experiences. The denial also erases their stories of suffering from public discourse and incorrectly suggests that environmental harms are evenly distributed, when in fact entire neighborhoods endure disproportionate levels of toxic pollution. Despite the extensive documentation of these inequities, the diffusion of responsibility allows systemic harm to take root, as people become indifferent to environmental assaults and accountability remains elusive. To engage in peaceful civic unrest, residents frequently turn to the legal system to seek redress for unsafe and unhealthy conditions.

The legal standards required to assign culpability in environmental racism cases are often exceptionally stringent, creating substantial barriers for communities seeking justice.[141] Even when clear patterns of discrimination are evident in the data, they rarely meet the narrow evidentiary thresholds required by the courts. The burden of proof in EJ cases typically rests on the residents living amid polluted landscapes. Those individuals often lack the financial resources and time needed to obtain legal representation. Additionally, intent can be nearly impossible to prove when structures of inequality and the racialized impact of policies are often hidden beneath bureaucratic procedures, zoning codes, or "colorblind" language.

Legal disenfranchisement has long reinforced the perception of African Americans as second-class citizens, sanctioning policies and practices that devalue Black lives. Rooted in economic exploitation and discriminatory land-use decisions that designate minority communities as acceptable locations for environmentally hazardous activity, the siting of hazardous facilities reflects this history. The consequences are far-reaching, producing higher rates of asthma, cancer, cardiovascular disease, and other toxin-induced illnesses.[142] Epidemiological and public health research further reveal that proximity to such facilities contributes to long-term genetic, neurological, and reproductive risks, as well as developmental disorders, particularly among children.[143] Even modest regulatory protections, when delayed or absent, can produce irreversible physiological damage.

Harriet A. Washington, the acclaimed American writer, scholar, and researcher whose groundbreaking scientific work lies at the critical intersection of race and biomedical ethics, is an influential voice within the EJ movement. Washington maintains that marginalized and vulnerable groups are disproportionately and deliberately affected due to the intentional, targeted assaults inflicted on their communities.[144] She firmly corroborates that this disturbing pattern of toxic exposure is not accidental, but deliberate and firmly entrenched in racial discrimination.[145] Furthermore, Washington asserts, while it is true that all Americans face some level of exposure to toxic pollutants, the degree, intensity, and duration of exposure experienced by minority populations are often significantly downplayed or even overlooked entirely by both mainstream media outlets and many sectors of the scientific community.[146] This widespread collective denial and underreporting not only conceals the full scope of environmental injustice, but also serves to exacerbate the racial trauma endured by affected communities.

It is not uncommon to come across statements from corporate spokesmen and government officials that blame toxic poisoning and other severe environmental maladies on the supposed pathology or inherent characteristics of a particular racial group. Scapegoating shifts responsibility away from the sources of pollution and instead places the burden on the victims themselves. The continuation of harmful tropes provides a convenient excuse to avoid transparency and ethical obligation for corrective action. Such narratives effectively mask the causes of environmental injustice, allowing polluters to continue their activities with little pressure for reform. Yet despite the perception that African Americans are apathetic toward environmental concerns, six out of ten individuals surveyed were actively involved in some form of activism to debunk this narrative and advance the EJ movement.[147]

Any serious effort to dismantle environmental racism requires not only legal reform and stricter protections, but also a recognition of the structural and systemic violence that maintains the prevailing racial order. Ultimately, if nothing is done, the cycle of environmental conflict strengthens polluters' ability to disenfranchise whole communities while creating generations of poverty traps for minoritized populations.[148] Without sustained intervention, the intertwined legacies of environmental harm and systemic racism will continue to perpetuate inequality, making meaningful change more difficult to achieve.

Grassroots resistance remains the most potent force for genuine change. Community organizations must continue monitoring pollution, conducting independent health studies, and challenging permits through legal and political channels.[149] From this vantage point, the EJ movement is both a civil rights effort and a peace movement in its truest sense.[150] It calls for the dismantling of violence integrated in the social order and the creation of conditions that allow all people to flourish. The alignment between Galtung's structural violence theory and EJ activism underscores a shared belief that peace is inseparable from justice, and justice cannot exist amid systemic harm.[151]

Although it may seem unconventional to propose that grassroots and EJ advocates engage with peace and conflict experts, the ingrained nature of environmental racism in American culture necessitates a multifaceted strategy for meaningful resistance. Therefore, those who are actively involved, or aspire to get involved, could benefit from collaborating more closely with conflict resolution practitioners. Legacy theorists such as Johan Galtung and Dennis Sandole are just a few in a long line of thought leaders who have developed frameworks to help examine the complexities that exist related to multiracial dynamics. Utilizing these frameworks would be advantageous in EJ cases involving multiple stakeholders when community distrust has taken shape, and divergent and conflicting interests exist. Advocates can leverage these foundational insights to provide a holistic perspective that would strengthen negotiations with government agencies, corporate representatives, and community members. While the goal is always to empower communities facing systemic barriers, there is an opportunity to increase the chances of securing durable policy reform that protects underserved populations. Structural violence is a map of risk and relief that ends at real doorsteps. It runs through codes and enforcement gaps to South Dallas's Shingle Mountain, Flint's poisoned taps, Port Arthur's fence-line blocks, and Louisiana's Cancer Alley—places where policy perpetuates the daily exposure to hazardous emissions and where residents demand a different future.

PART II

Cases of Injustice

"Injustice anywhere is a threat to justice everywhere."[152]

~ Dr. Martin Luther King Jr. (1929–1968)

Nobel Peace Prize Laureate; Renowned Leader of the American Civil Rights Movement

CHAPTER FOUR

Shingle Mountain

> "Residents who dared to fight for their right to a safe, clean environment were often accused of overreacting, of being uneducated or uninformed, and sometimes even of being racist themselves for pointing out the role of race in the siting of hazardous facilities."[153]

~ Dr. Dorceta Taylor

American Environmental Sociologist

Wangari Maathai Professor of Environmental Sociology and Senior Associate Dean of Diversity, Equity, and Inclusion at the Yale School of the Environment

In January 2018, a massive pile of discarded asphalt shingles began to rise in the Floral Farms neighborhood of southeast Dallas. Within months, the heap grew into what locals dubbed "Shingle Mountain,"[154] a sixty-foot mound of toxic roofing material deposited illegally by a recycling company. Its sudden appearance transformed the lives of nearby residents, who were forced to endure daily exposure to airborne pollutants, constant noise, and health risks. For Marsha Jackson, whose home was just steps away from the dump, the crisis would define years of her life and spark a broader struggle for environmental justice in Dallas.

This case is not simply about a pile of waste. It is a story about how environmental racism operates through legacy zoning, regulatory neglect, and political inaction. Shingle Mountain illustrates the lived experience of those Black and Latino communities that are disproportionately exposed to environmental hazards. The story of Marsha Jackson and her neighbors shows both the devastating human cost of systemic neglect and the power of grassroots advocacy in demanding accountability.

The Floral Farms neighborhood lies near Joppa, one of Dallas's most historically significant African American freedmen's communities. Joppa was founded in 1872 by formerly enslaved people who sought safety, land ownership, and self-determination.[155] Like many freedmen's towns across the South, Joppa was geographically isolated by design. This deliberate separation not only preserved the community's distinct cultural identity but also created vulnerabilities that would later be exploited. Over time, the same isolation that fostered self-sufficiency made Joppa an easy target for toxic land use and waste dumping, as railroads and heavy industry closed in around it, restricting economic opportunity and exposing residents to industrial pollution.

By the late twentieth century, Floral Farms—home to just over 150 residents—was a modest but close-knit neighborhood. Its population was predominantly African American and Hispanic, with many Latino residents primarily speaking Spanish.[156] In this family-oriented section of Dallas, residents were actively involved in churches and civic organizations, and they maintained strong social ties. Many families raised livestock on small plots, and children regularly played outdoors. Locals valued the area for its affordability, semirural character, and proximity to jobs in the city; however, a critical zoning policy enacted in the mid-1980s altered the community's fate. The policy created a loophole that allowed industrial operations to encroach on residential land, paving the way for environmental exploitation.

Marsha Jackson moved to Floral Farms in 1995, drawn by the opportunity to keep horses on her own land and raise her grandchildren in a quiet environment. After a long career at AT&T, she found peace in the neighborhood's exurban character. "I loved that I could raise my kids and grandkids around animals, and it was safe," she recalled.[157] For more than two decades, life in Floral Farms was stable. Residents were aware of the area's unusual land-use mix, with agricultural plots sitting beside industrial tracts, but few suspected how dramatically that would shape their future. As it turns out, the City of Dallas had quietly rezoned the area for heavy industry back in 1985,[158] a decision that was made without public consultation or notification. Residents purchasing property were never explicitly informed. In fact, for years, the designation lay dormant, buried in planning documents and invisible in ordinary routines.

On January 1, 2018, Jackson received a knock on her door. A new company, Blue Star Recycling, was interested in buying up local homes. When she declined, they assured her they would be "good neighbors" and promised to recycle the roofing material safely.[159] In reality, the company operated without a proper permit and quickly amassed a pile of roofing debris that towered over Jackson's property.[160] Within weeks, trucks began arriving at dawn, delivering load after load of asphalt shingles. The material—jagged, dusty, and toxic—piled into a growing heap less than fifty feet from Jackson's bedroom window. The shingles eventually accumulated into more than 70,000 tons of asphalt roofing debris, spread across more than 2.5 acres.[161] Jackson saw the dump grow. "It was huge, taller than my roof, in just days," she later recalled.[162]

The air filled with toxic particles as workers ground shingles into dust. The consequences were immediate. Residents began coughing, sneezing, and spitting up black phlegm. Jackson suffered respiratory problems and eventually permanent damage to her vocal cords, leaving her voice raspy and strained. She visited doctors repeatedly, often receiving steroid injections to combat inflammation. Over time, her vocal cords sustained permanent damage from inhaling fiberglass dust. "My voice will never be the same," she explained.[163]

Scientific studies confirm the health hazards residents described. Asphalt shingles contain fiberglass, petroleum hydrocarbons, silica, and heavy metals. When ground into dust, these substances release toxins that affect the respiratory, gastrointestinal, and cardiovascular systems. Long-term exposure to fine particulate matter increases risks of asthma, lung cancer, cardiovascular disease, and neurological disorders.[164] Unlike larger particles that the body can often cough or sneeze out, $PM_{2.5}$ (defined as particulate matter with a diameter of 2.5 microns or less) evades the body's natural defense mechanisms. Once inside, these microscopic pollutants travel through the bloodstream, causing inflammation in distant organs, accelerating plaque buildup in arteries, and disrupting oxygen delivery to brain tissues. Such microscopic invaders effectively poison multiple organ systems simultaneously, making them among the most insidious forms of pollution released by industry.[165]

But the contamination was not limited to the air. Rainfall carried the toxins into the soil and water, leaving behind residues of lead and other heavy metals. Even after the pile's removal, testing revealed lead concentrations of 1,450 parts per million (ppm), far exceeding the EPA's safety threshold of 200 ppm.[166] Adding to the devastation, the runoff from the mountain clogged a nearby creek, causing flooding that killed two horses belonging to a neighbor—a loss that highlighted both the environmental and emotional costs of the dump. What had once been a community where children played and animals thrived became a polluted, hazardous zone.

Children bore an especially heavy burden. Kept indoors for safety, they lost access to play, animals, and fresh air. Jackson compared their confinement to the isolation many experienced during the COVID-19 pandemic but emphasized that her community had been living this way long before.[167] The emotional toll on families was immense, with children suffering not only health consequences but also the loss of normal childhood experiences. Elderly residents were also vulnerable, with many reporting headaches and difficulty breathing. The noise and dust were constant, robbing the community of peace and health.

At first, Jackson fought alone. Many of her Latino neighbors feared retaliation due to immigration concerns. They urged Jackson to take the lead. "They told me, 'You be the spokesperson,' and I accepted that because I knew we had to speak up," she explained.[168] Initially, Jackson thought the city would intervene quickly. She began calling city offices daily, sending emails, filing complaints, and demanding inspections.

City officials promised to send inspectors, but no meaningful action followed. Months passed, and the pile continued to grow.

At the state level, the Texas Commission on Environmental Quality (TCEQ) proved ineffective. Jackson's complaints went unanswered. When she confronted regional officials directly, they admitted knowing about the site, but they failed to act. TCEQ eventually pursued enforcement against Blue Star Recycling for failing to maintain required hazard-management protections, a penalty Jackson described as meaningless compared to the harm inflicted. Although the area sat near a federal Superfund site—locations the EPA designates as among the nation's most contaminated—federal involvement was limited. Under the EPA's lead-regulator policy, primary responsibility for oversight was deferred to state regulators, leaving residents without direct federal assistance.[169] Instead of protecting residents, agencies debated jurisdiction and issued minimal fines.

Perhaps most devastating for Jackson was the lack of support from elected officials. Despite being represented by Black city council members and state legislators, she received little help. "None of them supported me," she said bluntly.[170] Only after a Dallas County commissioner wrote a letter in 2019 did her city council member take notice. Even then, the response was minimal. This neglect underscores how political disempowerment compounds environmental racism. Communities of color are not only exposed to disproportionate environmental burdens but also excluded from the political advocacy and protection enjoyed by wealthier neighborhoods.

Frustrated, Jackson attended community meetings and connected with local activists. In one meeting, she met allies who introduced her to *Dallas Morning News* columnist Robert Wilonsky. His reporting brought widespread attention to the crisis, with more than sixteen articles documenting the city's failure to act.[171] Through a series of exposés featuring photographs, Jackson's testimony, and sharp analysis of regulatory breakdowns, Wilonsky revealed how Shingle Mountain had been allowed to grow unchecked. He underscored the divide between wealthier neighborhoods, where such an operation would never be tolerated, and communities like Floral Farms, where protections failed.

The coverage sparked citywide outrage. Residents across Dallas demanded answers from the city council, questioning how such a blatant violation of health and zoning laws could continue unchecked. As media coverage grew, national figures took notice. Journalist Soledad O'Brien visited the site and featured Shingle Mountain in her documentary series, amplifying the outrage.[172] The image of O'Brien standing beside the towering mountain shocked viewers across the country. Faith leaders, civil rights groups, and allies across racial lines rallied to Jackson's cause. With each article and broadcast, pressure mounted on city leaders to act. It was only after the media spotlight that the City of Dallas filed suit against Blue Star in December 2018. Litigation dragged on for nearly a year. Trucks stopped arriving, but the mountain remained.

In 2019, a state judge ordered Christopher Ganter, proprietor of Blue Star Recycling, to undertake the large and costly task of hauling away the debris to clean up Shingle Mountain. Ganter, who resided in Collin County—a considerably more affluent area north of Dallas—claimed he could not afford the estimated half-million-dollar cost of the cleanup. Instead of complying with the court's directive, he filed for bankruptcy,[173] a legal strategy that effectively delayed the removal process and complicated the City of Dallas's efforts to hold him accountable. Bankruptcy maneuvers highlight a common challenge whereby business owners use financial insolvency as a shield against costly remediation.

Responsibility for the site eventually extended to the property owner, C.C. Rentals, which was named along with Blue Star Recycling in legal actions brought by the City of Dallas over the violations and cleanup costs.[174] In early 2021, the city also awarded a contract of $453,000 to a private company for the cleanup.[175] Unfortunately, the cleanup was incomplete. Even as legal settlements were reached and partial cleanup efforts began, lead contamination remained in the soil, and a large man-made pond formed on the site, raising fears of ongoing leaching into the groundwater. The aftermath continued to unfold, revealing unabated environmental hazards and health impacts that had already begun to manifest.

The truth was that Jackson and her neighbors had endured chronic exposure to particulate matter and toxic emissions resulting from the illegal dumping. According to research cited by the University of Texas Southwestern Medical Center, this exposure may have reduced life expectancy in the surrounding community.[176] Long-term contact with environmental pollutants can alter gene expression, leading to diseases that span generations, a dire prospect for communities already burdened by risk factors. Advances in the field of epigenetics reveal that environmental toxins do not solely affect those directly exposed;

they can trigger molecular changes in DNA regulation that impact children and grandchildren.[177] These epigenetic shifts may increase susceptibility to asthma, cancer, metabolic disorders, and neurodevelopmental conditions in future generations.[178]

Despite the prognosis, the community refused to be defined by the damage. Jackson ultimately cofounded Southern Sector Rising, a grassroots coalition advocating for environmental justice. The group organizes protests, holds public meetings, and builds alliances with churches, activists, and environmental groups. Their advocacy extends beyond Shingle Mountain to address batch plants, salvage yards, and other polluting industries that disproportionately target Dallas's southern, majority-Black and Latino neighborhoods.[179]

The Shingle Mountain crisis exposed deep flaws in both local and state governance. Rather than waiting for further intervention, Jackson and her allies turned their attention toward long-term change. What began as a fight against environmental neglect evolved into a broader movement for justice, healing, and renewal. They advocated for rezoning Floral Farms to prohibit future polluting industries, successfully lobbying for new land-use protections, which were approved in 2025.[180] They also pushed for the creation of a park, a green space co-designed by residents with input from pro bono architects, symbolizing their vision of reclaiming the neighborhood for families and children.

For Jackson, the question she hears most often is this: "Why didn't you just move?" Her answer reveals the injustice at the heart of the issue. "Why should I move when I was here first? What's wrong with regulating companies to follow the law and protect residents?"[181] Expecting families to uproot themselves because of illegal corporate actions shifts responsibility away from polluters and governments and onto victims.

The Floral Farms community demonstrates resilience and resistance in the face of systemic harm. By organizing, building coalitions, and demanding accountability, they transformed their suffering into a platform for reform. Their advocacy linked local struggles to national movements for environmental justice, proving that amplified voices can challenge entrenched systems. Shingle Mountain is gone, but its legacy remains. The pile of shingles may have been hauled away, but the contamination, health consequences, and psychological scars endure. Nevertheless, with unwavering resolve, Jackson fought for her family and neighbors to expose the systemic nature of environmental racism in Dallas. She showed that community advocacy can challenge powerful interests and push cities toward reform. For policymakers and advocates, Shingle Mountain is both a warning and a call to action, but it also reveals the possibility of transformation when communities resist. As Jackson herself put it, "Environmental injustice is real. We have the right to clean air and I will keep fighting so no other community has to go through what we did."[182]

CHAPTER FIVE

The Flint Water Crisis

"Flint falls right into the American narrative of cheapening Black life. White America may not have seen the common thread between Flint history and these tragedies, but Black America saw it immediately. That the blood of African-American children was unnecessarily and callously laced with lead speaks in the same rhythm as Black Lives Matter, a movement also born from the blood of innocent African Americans." [183]

~ Dr. Mona Hanna-Attisha

Associate Dean for Public Health and C.S. Mott Endowed Professor of Public Health at the Michigan State University College of Human Medicine

UP UNTIL THE LATE 1970s, Flint was a booming metropolis where tens of thousands of people worked in the automobile industry. It boasted a population of nearly 200,000 residents, supported flourishing automotive factories, and was home to the United Automobile Workers (UAW), General Motors (GM), and Mass Credit: The city was a lively and economically thriving industrialized town. GM alone employed over 80,000 people, making Flint one of the most prosperous cities in the United States at its peak.

Although GM started relocating its operations out of Flint nearly forty years earlier, it wasn't until the 1980s and 1990s that workers began to see a cascade of plant closures and downsizing. As GM continued to strategically move its operations, the city's economy saw a significant loss in tax revenue, triggering a crippling economic downturn. With a shrinking job market, industrial disinvestment, and high unemployment rates, the economic situation in Flint became even more dire. Those with the financial means moved out of the city into nearby suburbs and beyond, leaving behind a population of people who found it cost-prohibitive to uproot themselves and resettle elsewhere.

By the 2000s, Flint's population had decreased by half—from approximately 200,000 in 1960[184] to 81,000 in 2020—with mostly Black and low-income residents remaining. Of the 81,000 residents, roughly 57% identified as Black or African American, and an estimated 41% were living below the poverty line.[185] As such, the city saw a rise in low-income minority communities that were deemed unsafe and undesirable. According to a 2016 CNN investigative article by Sara Ganim and Linh Tran, "fifteen percent of the homes [were] boarded up and abandoned."[186] The article noted that the economic situation was so devastating that by 2011, Flint was in a fiscal emergency, prompting Michigan state officials to take control.

Facing a severe financial deficit from the years of disinvestment and neglect, the economic decline was felt across all of Flint's municipal operations. Most notably, its water-supply fund, which was in a $9 million hole. Maintenance of Flint's water system, which was originally built to serve an urban population of 200,000 residents, resulted in large fixed costs that were passed on to a diminishing customer base. This resulted in higher water rates compared to peer cities in Michigan. For those individuals already living in economic precarity, the increased water bills, which averaged over $50 per month, created additional financial strain. The city was on the brink of economic collapse with no money to replace its aging lead water pipes or support its large water system.

Under Michigan's emergency management law, then-Governor Rick Snyder appointed a succession of emergency managers to address Flint's financial shortfalls. In 2013, Darnell Earley replaced Michael Brown as emergency manager, and in 2014, Earley approved the switching of Flint's municipal water supply from Lake Huron—a pretreated water source—to the highly corrosive, untreated Flint River. In addition to being an untreated water source, the Flint River was known for being polluted due to years of human and industrial dumping from factories before they were shuttered.[187] Despite the known risks, the shift from Lake Huron was framed by Flint's unelected, state-appointed officials as a temporary cost-saving solution while construction for a new pipeline to Lake Huron was underway. The switch was anticipated to save the city an estimated $5 million over a two-year time frame. In theory, it would function as a short-term, low-cost substitute; in practice, it would become known as one of the most egregious environmental injustice cases in the twenty-first century, exposing Flint's residents to highly toxic, contaminated water.

The Flint water crisis was largely preventable. Treating Flint's water with the proper corrosion-control chemicals would have come at a nominal cost of $140 a day. Flouting federal mandates, the state's emergency managers were fixated on cutting costs and chose to ignore the well-established regulatory requirement of adding essential corrosion-inhibiting chemicals, such as orthophosphate, to the water system before distribution. As a result, the corrosive content from the Flint River aggressively ate away at the interior of the city's aging lead water pipes, leaching lead into its drinking water.

The fallout from the switch was immediate. Residents reported discolored water flowing through the tap that smelled of chlorine and sewage, believed to contain human or animal feces.[188] At the same time, there were also widespread reports of illnesses, rashes, hair loss, tooth loss, and gastrointestinal issues. By the summer of 2014, the water tested positive for coliform bacteria, and residents of the city were under the first of several boil-water advisories for bathing, cooking, washing dishes, and brushing their teeth.[189] As the crisis worsened, additional health repercussions linked to the water included a Legionnaires' disease outbreak in 2014 and 2015, during which there were ninety-one reported cases and twelve fatalities.[190]

The water crisis was further exacerbated by oversight failures of regulatory agencies. The EPA, which had broad authority to require corrosion control and enforce standards of the Safe Drinking Water Act's Lead and Copper Rule, did not intervene. This was in spite of reports from independent research scientists who alerted the EPA to the water's high lead levels as early as February 2015. The federal agency could have required corrective action, but instead, it deferred to the Michigan Department of Environmental Quality (MDEQ) for oversight and remediation. It would later come to light that MDEQ officials actively withheld the true extent of contamination from the EPA, reporting only that the water met regulatory standards.

In October of 2015, the Genesee County Health Department became the first to declare a state of emergency and began distributing water filters and bottled water to Flint residents. Five point-of-distribution sites (PODS) were also set up where community members could pick up free resources, including water testing kits. That same year, the crisis became national news, and under public pressure and a scathing moral indictment of negligence, Flint officials switched the water back to the treated Lake Huron supply. In January of 2016, former President Barack Obama issued a federal declaration of emergency, activating aid from FEMA, the Centers for Disease Control and Prevention (CDC), and the U.S. Department of Health and Human Services (HHS). With more than $90 million in funding allocated from state and federal sources pouring in, Flint began replacing its lead pipes with steel. It would take nearly a decade, and in 2025, Flint officials announced the completion of its pipe replacement program.

Flint's upgrades included the replacement of all its aging service lines—a total of 11,000 lead pipes—which accounted for 97% of the city's necessary replacements and upgrades to water infrastructure. Despite the progress in replacing the pipes, Flint continues to see a population decline and remains one of the most impoverished cities in America. In 2023, with a population of slightly over 79,000 and a median household income of approximately $33,000,[191] persistent poverty still shapes the daily lives of Flint's residents. Yet the danger now is that America will treat Flint as a tragedy of the past, when in truth, its neighborhoods continue to bear the scars of systemic neglect.

The poisoning of Flint's water was not just about corroded pipes. It was about a broader pattern of chronic disinvestment in minority communities long segregated by redlining and discriminatory lending practices. Residents in Flint saw little improvement in the city's infrastructure over the years, which contributed to the water crisis. Vacant buildings became visible reminders of abandonment, while the deterioration of schools and parks reflected the city's financial decline. Dilapidated houses that were built before 1920 were poorly maintained, and neighborhoods with vacancy rates of over 50% were clear indicators of economic neglect and aging infrastructure. The lack of revitalization and economic development led to a perpetual cycle of unsafe living conditions, disproportionate health disparities, and policy decisions that entrenched neighborhood-level inequalities. State and local officials denied that race was a factor in the decision to distribute untreated water; however, with Flint's overwhelmingly African American population, civil rights advocates considered the water crisis the epitome of environmental racism.

The Michigan Civil Rights Commission's 2017 report, *The Flint Water Crisis: Systemic Racism Through the Lens of Flint*, described a comprehensive study of the Flint water crisis and highlighted the intersection between race and poverty as contributing factors to the decisions made by state officials.[192] The commission found that under similar situations, a crisis of this magnitude would not have occurred in a more affluent White community.[193] First, the local revenue in predominantly White communities, enriched by higher property and income taxes, would enable municipalities to manage their infrastructure needs effectively. Second, White communities tend to have greater political clout, and the EPA and other regulatory agencies have historically enforced environmental laws more consistently for those communities, ensuring clean drinking water and the safeguarding of their public health.

The crisis in Flint forced the nation to confront existing environmental inequities perpetuated by race and class. Despite the fallout from Flint prompting a multitude of congressional hearings and a call for legislative reforms to strengthen protections for public water, countless numbers of low-income majority-minority cities in the U.S. are still facing dire circumstances that are impacting their tap water.[194]

The decisions leading to environmental harm are not always overt acts of discrimination; instead, there is a form of implicit bias at play that shows up as delayed responses by governmental agencies and the dismissal of residents who dare to voice their concerns and complaints. Implicit bias, unconscious attitudes, and stereotypes that shape perception and behavior mean that the suffering of African American people is too often minimized or rationalized by those with authoritative powers, leading to a "benign neglect." Benign neglect is neither explicit nor openly hostile, but it helps explain why the failure to enforce regulatory standards left Flint's residents unprotected as American citizens and resulted in an environmental assault and a devaluation of Black lives.

This devaluation was felt acutely by residents like Cynthia Morris, a lifelong Flint resident and community advocate.[195] In an interview, Morris recounted her upbringing in Flint, where she was raised by her grandparents—Southern migrants who came to the city for manufacturing jobs that embodied the promise of upward mobility that once defined Flint. Morris described Flint in its heyday as a vibrant and safe place where children could walk to the store alone and families gathered for holidays in close-knit neighborhoods. Yet over time, she also witnessed the city's decline, the shuttering of factories, and the erosion of public trust.

Morris's personal journey, from teen mother to college graduate and CEO of a senior services organization, mirrors the resilience of Flint's residents. She spoke candidly about the exhaustion of working third-shift jobs while attending school full time and raising children. Her story is one of perseverance, but also of systemic barriers: As the first in her family to attend college, she navigated institutional bureaucracy without guidance and nearly dropped out before an adviser intervened. Her experience underscores the importance of support systems and the impact of structural neglect not just in infrastructure, but in education, healthcare, and opportunity.

When asked about the water crisis, Morris emphasized its impact on Flint's seniors, a demographic often overlooked in EJ conversations. "Everybody always forgets about the seniors," she said. "They're the ones who stayed. They're the ones who delivered water. They're the ones raising grandkids while parents are working multiple jobs."[196] Morris described the logistic challenges seniors faced—lifting heavy water cases, dealing with broken appliances from corrosive water, and suffering from dental and skin issues. Her organization launched "Senior

Lives Matter," a program focused on mental health and resource access for elderly residents affected by the crisis.

Morris also highlighted the uneven impact of the crisis across Flint's neighborhoods. "Some lead levels were higher in very strategic places," she noted, pointing to inner-city, low-income, predominantly Black areas as the most affected.[197] Her observations align with Dr. Mona Hanna-Attisha's research, which revealed that children in Flint's poorest neighborhoods—Wards 5, 6, and 7—had the highest blood lead levels.[198] These neighborhoods were not only physically neglected but structurally disadvantaged, with aging housing stock, high vacancy rates, and limited access to healthcare.

Dr. Hanna-Attisha's findings, published in the *American Journal of Public Health*, showed that lead exposure in Flint doubled and even tripled in some areas after the water switch.[199] Her research confirmed what residents like Morris already knew. The crisis was not random; it was concentrated in communities of color. The long-term effects on children are staggering, with thousands exposed to neurotoxic levels of lead.[200] Even trace amounts can cause irreversible damage, including lower IQ, developmental delays, and behavioral disorders. These outcomes are compounded by preexisting socioeconomic disadvantages, making recovery even more difficult.

Morris witnessed the political dysfunction that followed the crisis. She described city council meetings filled with anger and distrust, where residents demanded accountability but were met with infighting and gridlock. "People are tired," she said. "They just want results."[201] Her comments reflect a broader sentiment in Flint. A desire for healing, for justice, and for meaningful change.

The Flint water crisis is often framed as a failure of infrastructure, but it is also a failure of democracy. The use of emergency managers, the dismissal of community voices, and the delayed response from regulatory agencies all point to a system that prioritizes control over care. Morris's story, like those of many Flint residents, reveals the human cost of this failure. Hers is a story of resilience, but also of pain, a reminder that environmental justice begins with the lived experiences of those most affected.

As Flint continues to rebuild, the voices of residents like Cynthia Morris must guide the process. Their insights, their advocacy, and their firsthand knowledge are invaluable. Environmental justice is not just about clean water; it is about dignity, equity, and the right to thrive. Flint's story is far from over, and its lessons must inform how we protect and empower communities across the nation.

CHAPTER SIX

Port Arthur's "Belly of the Beast"

"Ending pollution means forcing powerful industries to act against their financial interests, and this cannot be accomplished by individuals. It is the responsibility of our government, including the EPA and the public health professionals that advise them, to eradicate untested, underregulated poisons from residential housing, schools, and fence-line industries."[202]

~ Harriet A. Washington

Medical Ethicist, Scholar, and Writer

Author of *A Terrible Thing to Waste: Environmental Racism and Its Assault on the American Mind* and *Medical Apartheid*; Fellow at Harvard Medical School, the National Center for Bioethics at Tuskegee University, and Columbia University's School of Journalism

PORT ARTHUR, TEXAS, SITS on the Gulf Coast near the Louisiana border, approximately ninety miles east of Houston. With a population of roughly 56,000, the city has long been defined by its proximity to oil refineries and petrochemical plants. These facilities, which began rising during the oil boom of the early 1900s, have shaped the city's identity for more than a century. Among the earliest was a major refinery opened in 1903 by Texaco, originally known as The Texas Fuel Company.

Port Arthur's industrial identity is inseparable from its economic history. The city's proximity to deep waterways and shipping routes made it a strategic hub for energy and petrochemical development. The founder, Arthur Stilwell, envisioned Port Arthur as a terminus for his railroad, but wary of Galveston's hurricane vulnerability, he chose to build inland and dig a ship channel to the Gulf. That decision laid the groundwork for the city's transformation into a refining powerhouse.[203] Its maritime access and central role in the national energy supply chain attract multinational investment and sustained federal infrastructure support, shaping both the city's growth and its vulnerabilities.

Today, Port Arthur remains home to one of North America's largest oil refineries. Operated by Motiva Enterprises, the Port Arthur Refinery is capable of processing 720,000 barrels of crude oil per day.[204] It is for this reason that the community, situated at the very heart of America's petrochemical empire, has become known as "the belly of the beast." The phrase captures both its geographic reality and its symbolic weight as a place where the machinery of energy production operates in plain view of homes, schools, and churches. It is also a place where residents live with the constant trade-off between economic survival and environmental sacrifice.

Although industrial activity in the city has generated jobs and economic activity, it has imposed a heavy environmental toll on nearby neighborhoods. Residents contend with chronic exposure to harmful emissions, including sulfur dioxide (SO_2), hydrogen sulfide (H_2S), and fine particulate matter ($PM_{2.5}$). The city's industrial infrastructure is surrounded by more than six major chemical and petrochemical facilities, including the

Oxbow Calcining plant, BASF's steam cracker facility, the refineries operated by Motiva, Valero, and TotalEnergies, and the Chevron Phillips Chemical plant.

John Beard Jr., a lifelong resident and former city council member, recalls the pervasive stench of rotten eggs, a byproduct of industrial emissions. "I've come to learn and realize that it's the smell of death," he said. His father, who worked in the local industry, once told him, "Don't turn up your nose at that smell. It's the smell of money."[205]

The environmental burden in Port Arthur is not hidden; it is felt every day. Residents describe the air as thick, foul-smelling, and sometimes visible. "You can't sit outside anymore because you can't stand to smell the air," said longtime resident Diane Jackson. "Sometimes, if you sit outside long enough, you'll see black stuff all over the cars." Her husband and neighbors, she recalled, would cough up thick white mucus, which she attributed to the pollution.[206]

This firsthand account is echoed by Beard, who worked for ExxonMobil for thirty years. "If you parachuted in and asked someone if they knew anyone who had cancer or died from it, you wouldn't find a single person who didn't," he said.[207] Beard's own family has suffered from respiratory issues and allergies, and he describes the sensation of breathing the air "like drinking something too hot. It burns the roof of your mouth."[208]

Beard, who founded the Port Arthur Community Action Network (PACAN), has been at the forefront of challenging regulatory failures. "We're not just an environmental organization," he explained. "We're about community development and improving quality of life. If you improve the environment, you improve people's health,"[209] a truth residents of West Port Arthur know all too well.

West Port Arthur, a predominantly Black and low-income community, lies directly adjacent to the Oxbow Calcining plant. This facility emits over twenty-two million pounds of sulfur dioxide annually, accounting for approximately 90% of Jefferson County's SO_2 emissions.[210] Despite national air quality standards, emissions from Oxbow have remained largely unchanged for nearly a decade.

The Texas Commission on Environmental Quality (TCEQ), the state agency responsible for regulating air and water quality, has repeatedly renewed Oxbow's operating permits despite ongoing community concerns and a history of air-pollution issues at the facility. Notably, in 2020, TCEQ renewed Oxbow's federal operating permit even as public records and monitoring data showed exceedances of sulfur dioxide and other pollutants in prior years.[211]

Despite staggering pollution levels, facilities like Oxbow Calcining continue to operate without modern pollution controls. Under the Clean Air Act, older plants are exempt from installing technologies such as scrubbers unless they undergo major physical modifications.[212] Because Oxbow has never undertaken such an upgrade, it remains classified as an existing source and is therefore not required to install these controls.[213] This regulatory loophole has allowed the facility to avoid compliance with stricter standards. The company, owned by billionaire William Koch, has cited the cost of installing scrubbers—"an estimated $56 million to install the scrubbers and $10 million to operate them"—as unjustifiable, claiming there is "no payback potential except environmental compliance."[214]

In 2021, Lone Star Legal Aid and the Environmental Integrity Project filed an eighty-four-page petition on behalf of PACAN, requesting a federal investigation into TCEQ's renewal of Oxbow's operating permit. The petition argued that the state agency failed to ensure compliance with National Ambient Air Quality Standards and ignored evidence of emission exceedances.[215] It also claimed that TCEQ neglected to conduct a formal disparate impact analysis, despite the fact that West Port Arthur is 98% people of color, with over 60% living below the poverty line.[216]

The EPA launched an investigation into potential Title VI violations of the Civil Rights Act, marking a rare federal acknowledgment of environmental racism. However, the agency ultimately concluded that there was insufficient evidence to prove discriminatory intent, a legal standard notoriously difficult to meet.[217] Beard remains undeterred. "We're going to get epidemiological studies, case studies, and anecdotal evidence to focus on the problem and its cause," he said. "I see a path forward."[218]

Although the Oxbow case is significant, it is only one facet of the wider industrial pressures confronting Port Arthur's neighborhoods. Residents have long organized against the expansion of industrial facilities that encroach on their local surroundings. One particularly egregious example involved the construction of a tank farm with over thirty storage tanks, just steps from residents' front doors. The project was approved without meaningful community consultation. When residents voiced concerns, company representatives advised them to take their grievances to the city council, which had already approved the zoning. "They must think we're stupid,"[219] one homeowner remarked, pointing to the broader pattern of deflection and dismissiveness from industry and city officials.

The company's response was to host a barbecue. Many saw the gesture as a superficial attempt to pacify dissent. Anne Robinson, a lifelong resident, was outraged. "You're polluting our neighborhood, and you invite us to a barbecue? Why don't you throw in a couple of watermelons while you're at it?" she said. Her frustration was compounded when company representatives later attempted to intimidate her for speaking to the press.[220]

These tactics, token gestures followed by suppression, are not unique to Port Arthur. Across the country, residents of fence-line communities report similar experiences: intimidation, threats, and harassment when challenging industrial pollution. Beard described the atmosphere as one of fear and compliance, saying, "You can't do this to people."[221]

PACAN has taken a proactive stance, commissioning air quality studies and participating in administrative hearings to challenge new permits. In one case, Beard successfully argued for standing in a hearing against Sempra LNG's proposed expansion. "They tried to say I wasn't affected any more than anyone else," he recalled. "But that's a tacit admission that it affects us all."[222] To Beard, it confirmed what residents had long understood. No one is exempt from the impact.

The fight for accountability is ongoing. Residents continue to report elevated rates of asthma, cancer, and heart disease—conditions linked to long-term exposure to pollutants such as sulfur dioxide and benzene. Yet despite public pressure and federal investigations, meaningful regulatory reform remains elusive. At the same time, residents found themselves confronting two intertwined struggles of environmental injustice and economic dependence. The very industries that harmed the community also sustained it. For decades, steady refinery jobs masked the accumulating toll of pollution, creating a sense of progress built on unequal sacrifice. But as hiring practices shifted away from local residents, people were left with fewer opportunities and the same—or even greater—environmental burdens.

For many families, the refineries offered economic mobility. Beard's father worked for Gulf Oil for over forty-four years, securing a stable livelihood that allowed Beard to attend college and raise his own family. "That opportunity paid itself forward through three generations," he said.[223] However, Beard himself witnessed the shift from community-based employment to outsourced labor and automation.

In the past, refinery jobs were plentiful and well paying. "You got one of those jobs, you had a job for life," Beard recalled.[224] But today, the workforce has been dramatically reduced. Motiva and Valero, once employing nearly 10,000 people combined, now operate with fewer than 5,000 employees. Contract labor has replaced local hires, and many contractors commute from outside the city. "The industry has changed in ways that have adversely affected the city," Beard said.[225] As these jobs disappeared, so did the economic stability they once provided, leaving Port Arthur with high unemployment and persistent poverty.

This economic vulnerability was compounded by the city's racial geography. West Port Arthur was deliberately designed with small lots and minimal infrastructure to restrict expansion. "They built shotgun houses on twenty-five-foot lots so Black folks wouldn't move into White neighborhoods," Beard explained.[226] Many of these homes still stand, some rebuilt after hurricanes with little improvement. The city's history of segregation and exclusion is etched into its landscape. Beard described how Black residents were confined to specific areas and given limited access to public amenities up until the mid-1950s. "We had one park we could go to, and even that was on 'Black Day,' the one day we were allowed," he said.[227] These patterns of spatial and economic marginalization continue to shape the social conditions of those who call the city home.

Port Arthur stands as a stark example of environmental racism, where industrial expansion and regulatory neglect converge to burden communities of color with disproportionate health risks. The city's legacy of petrochemical development has created a landscape where economic opportunity and environmental harm are deeply intertwined. For residents like Beard, the fight is not just about pollution; it is about dignity, justice, and survival.

Despite decades of exposure to toxic emissions, regulatory agencies have failed to enforce meaningful protections. Loopholes in the Clean Air Act, lenient permitting practices, and corporate influence have allowed facilities to operate without accountability. "We've relied on others for so long and haven't gotten very far," Beard remarked. "Sometimes you have to look within to do for yourself."[228]

The path forward requires more than federal investigations or symbolic gestures. It demands systemic change, rigorous enforcement of environmental standards, closure of regulatory loopholes, and genuine community engagement. It also requires a legal framework that can address disparate impact, not just discriminatory intent, to ensure that communities like West Port Arthur are no longer sacrificed for industrial gain.

Environmental justice advocates, policymakers, and the general public must recognize Port Arthur as part of a broader national pattern of environmental inequity. The city's story is a call to action. It is a reminder that clean air, safe neighborhoods, and equitable development are not privileges, but rights. As Beard put it, "So long as they're polluting, I'm gonna be here fighting."[229] His challenge to Sempra LNG's expansion permit emphasized how difficult it is for residents to gain meaningful participation in environmental hearings, where demonstrating direct harm is often required before community voices are fully considered. The process illuminated how proximity and exposure continue to shape who is allowed into the room and whose concerns carry weight. If such efforts were more widely supported, they could expand access to formal review processes for other fence-line communities, especially those historically sidelined by narrow definitions of legal injury. Yet without statutory reform or stronger federal oversight, the imbalance between industrial privilege and community protection is likely to endure. Port Arthur's experience offers a critical lens for evaluating how environmental justice can be integrated into national energy policy, not as an afterthought, but as a foundational concern.

CHAPTER SEVEN

South Baltimore's Silent Killers

"Everything shows that pollution does discriminate. We can determine almost how long you're going to live by your address, and the addresses of poor people and people of color are such that we live near the most dangerous polluting facilities."[230]

~ Dr. Beverly Wright

Founder and Executive Director of the Deep South Center for Environmental Justice; Professor of Sociology at Dillard University

BALTIMORE, ONCE BRANDED "THE City That Reads," stands at the intersection of industrial pollution and systemic poverty. This pairing fuels high rates of respiratory illness, widens health disparities, and drives premature death. The slogan, introduced by former Mayor Kurt Schmoke in 1988 to promote literacy, was aspirational at the time, when an estimated 200,000 adults in the city were considered functionally illiterate. While no longer used in official city branding, the phrase remains a cultural marker, reflecting both civic ambition and the challenges of educational equity.[231]

By the early 1900s, Baltimore's landscape was rapidly transforming. Developers converted farmland into dense grids of rowhouses, shaping the city's infrastructure. These homes housed generations of working families employed in shipyards, steel mills, factories, and port facilities. The city's economic identity became tightly bound to heavy industry, and its neighborhoods reflected the layout of a typical company town.

In 1910, Baltimore enacted the nation's first residential segregation ordinance, which prohibited Black residents from moving into majority-White blocks and vice versa. Although the Supreme Court declared such ordinances unconstitutional in 1917, the city continued to enforce racial boundaries through zoning, restrictive covenants, and real estate practices that defined the city's racial geography.[232] These policies laid the foundation for what Dr. Lawrence T. Brown calls the "Black Butterfly," a term describing the geographic pattern of racial segregation that developed in Baltimore, where majority-Black neighborhoods were on the eastern and western wings of the city, flanking the wealthier, Whiter central corridor known as the "White L."[233]

South Baltimore's waterfront neighborhoods—Mount Winans, Westport, Brooklyn, and Curtis Bay—have long been shaped by their proximity to heavy industry. Shipbuilding, steel fabrication, sugar refining, distilling, and later waste-to-energy and medical waste disposal were clustered along the Patapsco River. The operations generated employment but also left a residue of toxic exposure, noise, and risk. In these communities, residential blocks overlapped with rail yards, highways, and heavy industry, often without effective buffers or environmental protections.[234] Many African American families were confined to these neighborhoods, where industrial land uses multiplied and infrastructure decisions intensified divisions. Over time, zoning and permitting normalized environmental hazards near homes, schools, and parks. Today, these communities continue to bear a disproportionate burden of pollution and disinvestment—conditions that reflect not only historical injustice but also ongoing policy failures.

In the face of systemic neglect and environmental harm, South Baltimore residents have built powerful grassroots movements. At the center of this advocacy is Carol Williams, a longtime Westport resident whose leadership has helped galvanize community resistance and policy engagement. Williams's advocacy is rooted in her lived experience. She has spent over two decades in the neighborhood, witnessing its decline and fighting for its future. "It's sad to see how it just decayed because the resources would not come here," she said. "There was no one really advocating for us in the way they should have."[235] Reflecting on this dynamic, Williams explained, "There is this bizarre relationship between residential housing and heavy industry. Not just commercial, not just a car repair shop, I mean like a frickin' incinerator."[236] Williams was referring to two major incinerators located within Baltimore city: the WIN Waste facility in Westport and the Curtis Bay Energy medical waste incinerator. Their presence underscores both the bureaucratic indifference and the economic expediency that govern land use and public health.

The WIN Waste Innovations facility, formerly known as Wheelabrator Baltimore and BRESCO, has operated in South Baltimore's Westport neighborhood since 1985.[237] Originally built to address the city's growing solid waste needs, the incinerator burns up to 2,250 tons of municipal waste daily and converts it into energy.[238] While touted as a waste-to-energy solution, the facility has long been the city's largest single source of air pollution.[239] The incinerator emits fine particulate matter, nitrogen oxides, lead, and other toxins that contribute to respiratory illnesses—especially asthma.[240] "Why does everybody have asthma?" Carol Williams asked. "Why is everybody spitting as they walk down the street, trying to clear their throats? It's not just a bad habit; there's something behind that."[241]

Despite its environmental impact, the facility remains central to Baltimore's waste management system. It produces up to sixty megawatts of electricity, which is enough to power tens of thousands of homes.[242] Long-term contracts with the city, valued in the tens of millions of dollars, commit Baltimore to keeping the incinerator operational through 2031, with options to renew.[243] These agreements create significant financial and legal barriers to shutting it down, which communities must confront if they hope to reshape the city's approach to waste management.

In response, community groups have pushed for stricter emissions standards and greater transparency.[244] In 2019, the Baltimore Clean Air Act sought to enforce tighter pollution limits and real-time monitoring.[245] However, in 2020, a federal judge struck down the law, ruling that Baltimore could not exceed state-level air quality standards.[246] The decision effectively blocked local efforts to address health concerns tied to the incinerator and left residents without recourse to address the incinerator's health impacts. Williams described the incinerator as a symbol of environmental injustice. "They want to keep it as it is. It was there when you got there, what difference does it make?" she said, referring to how officials dismiss community concerns because of the incinerator's long-standing presence.[247] She added, "Just because it's been [there] doesn't mean it should stay. We need to change the rules," Williams asserted. "We want the same thing as everyone else. Clean, vibrant, healthy communities. We're not asking for luxury," she insisted. "We're asking for dignity for neighborhoods."[248]

Just seven miles south of the WIN Waste facility lies another environmental hazard—Curtis Bay Energy, the nation's largest medical waste incinerator.[249] Serving clients from nineteen states, the District of Columbia, and parts of Canada, the facility incinerates biomedical waste—including used syringes, contaminated garments, and infectious substances—from hospitals, nursing homes, and laboratories.[250] A Maryland Department of the Environment (MDE) investigation in 2019 found egregious violations, including mercury emissions that were 400 times the regulatory limit and practices that bypassed pollution control equipment.[251]

Curtis Bay is home to roughly 6,500 residents, 40% of whom live below the poverty line.[252] The incinerator sits disturbingly close to residential areas and waterways.[253] The 2019 MDE investigation found violations that included overloading incinerators, handling waste improperly, and concealing illegal sump pump activity during inspections.[254] In 2023, Curtis Bay Energy pled guilty to forty criminal counts and was ordered to pay $1.75 million in fines, including $750,000 for community environmental projects.[255] Under new ownership since 2021, Curtis Bay Energy has made partial infrastructure and compliance upgrades, but the cost of fully modernizing pollution controls would be significantly higher than the partial upgrades completed to date, revealing the gap between penalties and true accountability.[256] Despite these improvements, the incinerator continues to be a chronic source of emissions violations, underscoring its ongoing threat to public health and environmental safety.[257]

An epidemiological assessment in 2025 estimated $36.9 million in annual health damages from the Curtis Bay incinerator's emissions.[258] The costs include hospital visits, medication, lost productivity, and diminished quality of life. These figures align with longer-term observations in Baltimore that asthma-related hospitalizations declined after pollution controls were installed, then rose with lapses or violations.[259] Citywide, roughly one in five children has asthma—more than twice the national average—with even higher rates in predominantly Black neighborhoods.[260] Together, the WIN Waste incinerator and the Curtis Bay medical waste facility contribute significantly to the city's toxic burden, reinforcing the link between industrial emissions and Baltimore's severe asthma rates.[261]

Although the Curtis Bay facility is not designated as an EPA Superfund site, a classification typically reserved for abandoned or uncontrolled hazardous waste locations, it continues to operate under state-issued permits with limited federal oversight. Williams considers the medical waste incinerator the worst offender in Baltimore. "[Hospitals send all] their waste here. And we live with it."[262]

This local frustration emphasizes the broader legal complexities surrounding air quality regulation in South Baltimore. Under the federal Clean Air Act, state-issued Title V permits govern incinerators, with federally delegated oversight from the

EPA through MDE.²⁶³ The Baltimore Clean Air Act attempted to supplement that framework with local standards and transparency mandates. Although the law was ultimately invalidated, the push for stronger protections continued.²⁶⁴ In 2024, the South Baltimore Community Land Trust, the Chesapeake Bay Foundation, and the Environmental Integrity Project filed a Title VI civil rights complaint with the EPA, arguing that the city's ten-year solid waste plan perpetuates disparate impacts by relying on the waste-to-energy facility instead of accelerating alternatives.²⁶⁵ Because Baltimore's Department of Public Works receives federal funding, the complaint falls within EPA oversight—even after the Supreme Court's 2020 ruling in *Comcast Corp. v. National Association of African American-Owned Media*, which limited private Title VI suits.²⁶⁶ Federal agencies still retain the authority to investigate and enforce policies against practices that result in disparate impact.²⁶⁷

As of 2025, EPA review remained underway.²⁶⁸ Regardless of the outcome, the complaint articulates what many residents already know. The distribution of pollution is not random. It is patterned by race and class. Undoing that pattern requires more than vigilance over individual permits; it requires a plan to deconcentrate hazards, strengthen buffers, and restructure the city's approach to waste and freight so that disadvantaged neighborhoods are no longer the default site for the dirtiest work. Williams's diagnosis is blunt: "Environmental racism is a willful act. It's when people put things in communities that are damaging, knowing the people who live there can't fight back."²⁶⁹ This is not simply about oversight or neglect; it's about power. That imbalance shapes not only where pollution goes, but also who is able to resist it. The barriers to advocacy are steep, and for residents of South Baltimore, even showing up to fight back comes at a cost. Williams described the financial and emotional toll of civic engagement—taking time off work, paying for parking, printing materials, and attending meetings. "Advocating is expensive," she said. "I've blown enough vacation time that I don't get to go on [personal] trips. We expect [people] to work from 8 to 4:30, then feed their kids, and sit two hours at City Hall?!"[270] In a city where pollution is political, the pursuit of justice can feel impossible to attain.

Race and income also shape how voices are received in public forums. Williams's experience underscores how deeply embedded bias is in civic discourse. "My White colleague, they're going to pay attention to her a little more. I can go down there speaking the Queen's English, dressed in my Sunday best, and [they will still see me] as angry," she said.[271] These disparities in perception and influence are not incidental; they are structural. They reflect a system in which Whiteness and wealth confer legitimacy, while Black and working-class voices are often dismissed or pathologized. Even political representation does not guarantee accountability. Williams is candid in her critique of elected officials, including those from her own community, suggesting that campaign contributions from polluting industries often shape decisions behind closed doors. This dynamic reveals how environmental racism is sustained not only by historical zoning maps but also by contemporary political economies. In response, activists like Williams have turned to transparency and public pressure. They track campaign donations, attend hearings, and use social media to expose conflicts of interest. "I follow the money," Williams explained.[272] By tracing influence and exposing hidden ties, she hopes to expose corruption so resistance has a fighting chance.

South Baltimore's fight is not just local; it echoes across cities where Black and brown communities are targeted for industrial development and denied political voice. As Williams reminds us, "They count us out, but we're still here and we're not done."[273] The path forward demands more than policy tweaks. It requires zoning reform, transparent governance, and investment in community-led solutions. It calls for leaders who understand the lived realities of environmental harm and who are willing to act. "Some leaders don't even know what's happening," Williams said. "They need a GPS to get down here, but once they're here, they need to look around and act."[274]

South Baltimore's residents are doing their part. They have mapped the harms, negotiated agreements, stood up in hearings, and documented violations. They have organized across neighborhoods and partnered with researchers. They have imagined a city in which clean air and quiet nights are not zip-code privileges. The obligation now rests with the city and the state to replace permissive zoning with protective policy, to measure what matters in real time, and to align budgets with public health.

Baltimore's story is still being written. The question is whether the next chapter will continue to normalize harm in the same familiar places or finally deliver the equal protections that are promised by law. South Baltimore's silent killers have been named. The work ahead is to ensure that naming leads to action, and action leads to protection.

PART III

Activism, Resistance, and Resilience

"I have learned you are never too small to make a difference."[275]

~ Greta Thunberg

Climate and Environmental Activist; Founder of Fridays for Future; Advocate for Global Climate Action

CHAPTER EIGHT

Progress Since the Landmark 1987 Study

"The issue of environmental injustice in our communities has become an issue of life and death."[276]

~ **Dr. Benjamin Chavis**

Civil Rights Leader, Environmental Justice Advocate, and Ordained Minister

President and CEO of the National Newspaper Publishers Association; Former Executive Director of the NAACP; Former Executive Director of the United Church of Christ Commission for Racial Justice; Coauthor of the Landmark 1987 Report *Toxic Wastes and Race in the United States*

IN THE EARLY 1980s, the protests in Warren County, North Carolina, marked the beginning of what would become the modern environmental justice movement.[277] Residents, the majority of them Black, mobilized against the state's decision to locate a toxic PCB landfill in their community, drawing national attention to the racialized nature of environmental decision-making. It was during this movement that Dr. Benjamin Chavis, then serving as executive director of the United Church of Christ Commission for Racial Justice, coined the term "environmental racism." The phrase captured a truth long understood in marginalized communities. Race, more than class or geography, was the most consistent factor of environmental harm.

Building on that early foundation, in 1987 the United Church of Christ Commission for Racial Justice published *Toxic Wastes and Race in the United States*, a groundbreaking report that empirically demonstrated race to be the most significant factor in the siting of hazardous waste facilities.[278] This study marked the first time that environmental racism entered the mainstream of national policy conversations, linking civil rights with environmental protection. Using census tract–level data, the report revealed statistically significant patterns, showing that communities with higher percentages of African Americans were consistently more likely to host toxic waste sites than predominantly White communities.

Led by Dr. Benjamin Chavis and researcher Charles Lee, the study analyzed over 400 hazardous waste sites across the country. Their findings were backed by rigorous statistical analysis; multivariate modeling showed that the probability of these racial disparities occurring by chance was less than one in 10,000.[279] Based on the conclusion that these disparities were not random outcomes but the predictable results of systemic inequities in governance and enforcement, they called for urgent regulatory reforms and the elimination of discriminatory policies. This elevated the conversation from isolated protests to an evidence-based analysis, prompting hearings in Congress and sparking demands for governmental accountability.[280] Around the same time, Dr. Robert Bullard's research in Houston, later published as *Dumping in Dixie: Race, Class, and Environmental Quality*, provided further empirical evidence that race was the most significant predictor of exposure to environmental hazards.[281]

The impact was immediate and far-reaching. What had once been dismissed as local outcry from frontline neighborhoods was now recognized as a civil rights issue. The data gave moral and legal weight to demands for environmental protection and racial equity. Communities from Louisiana's Cancer Alley to Chicago's South Side began connecting their local struggles to this broader pattern.[282] Yet despite the visibility generated by the report, sustained policy action lagged behind. Federal and state agencies acknowledged the disproportionate environmental burdens borne by minority and low-income communities, yet enforcement was often delayed, diluted, or actively rolled back.

In response to this lack of meaningful reform, leaders and activists convened the First National People of Color Environmental Leadership Summit in Washington, D.C., in 1991.[283] The summit brought together more than 1,000 delegates, representing grassroots organizations, faith-based coalitions, scholars, and policymakers from across the country.[284] Out of this historic gathering emerged the "17 Principles of Environmental Justice," which articulated a comprehensive framework connecting environmental protection to housing, labor, health, land use, and self-determination.[285] The summit reframed environmental justice as a human rights issue rooted in community empowerment and collective sovereignty, laying the philosophical foundation for future federal action.

Following this wave of activism, the EPA took its first major step in 1992 by establishing the Office of Environmental Justice (OEJ).[286] The OEJ broadened its mandate beyond hazardous waste to include air and water quality, urban development, and other environmental challenges. Tools like EJSCREEN, an interactive mapping platform combining environmental and demographic data, helped identify high-burden communities and guide more equitable policy decisions.[287] Still, the absence of a fully integrated national database across federal, state, and local levels hindered (and continues to hinder) coordinated action.[288]

Then in 1993, the EPA created the National Environmental Justice Advisory Council (NEJAC) to provide structured, sustained input from affected communities and to advise the EPA Administrator on EJ policy.[289] Its diverse membership—spanning industry, academia, public health, nonprofit organizations, and grassroots leaders—ensured that environmental justice policy would be informed by a broad range of lived experiences and expertise.[290] NEJAC's role was further strengthened by President Clinton's 1994 Executive Order 12898, which directed all federal agencies to address disproportionately high environmental and health burdens in minority and low-income communities. But NEJAC's visibility and influence diminished significantly during the Trump administration, and the council was terminated in 2025.

While federal agencies were building advisory infrastructure, early legislative efforts to codify EJ principles into law faced significant resistance. In 1992, Senator Al Gore and Representative John Lewis introduced the Environmental Justice Act, which aimed to address and mitigate environmental threats in disadvantaged communities.[291] The bill never reached the floor for a vote, reflecting Congress's hesitancy to confront racialized environmental disparities directly. In 1994, Senator Paul Wellstone introduced a public health bill to prohibit discrimination in federally funded environmental programs. Like its predecessor, it stalled in Congress, a sign of the gap between institutional acknowledgment and legislative commitment.

Despite legislative setbacks, the groundwork laid by these efforts helped pave the way for Executive Order 12898, signed by President Bill Clinton on February 11, 1994.[292] Titled *Federal Actions to Address Environmental Justice in Minority Populations and Low-Income Populations*, the order directed all federal agencies to identify and address disproportionately high and adverse environmental and health effects of their programs on marginalized communities. It also mandated the creation of interagency working groups and required agencies to incorporate environmental justice into their missions.

Following this directive, the EPA strengthened its environmental justice infrastructure and expanded OEJ's role, developing tools for community engagement, grant programs, and data tracking to support fence-line communities affected by industrial pollution. However, as a presidential directive rather than legislation, the order lacked statutory authority and could not compel compliance. Many agencies treated compliance as discretionary, producing inconsistent results. The lack of a clear enforcement mechanism allowed polluting industries to continue operating in vulnerable communities with minimal oversight.[293]

In the absence of consistent federal enforcement, residents mobilized to fill the gaps. Led by grassroots organizations, local governments, and university-based research centers, these efforts transformed EJ from a national policy discussion into a lived practice of civic participation and legal advocacy.[294] In effect, local and state actors became the primary drivers of implementation, translating federal ideals into tangible change. California emerged as a leader, enacting CalEPA's Environmental Justice Program in 2000 and launching CalEnviroScreen, a mapping tool that integrated demographic, health, and pollution data to identify burdened communities.[295] New Jersey followed with the Environmental Justice Law of 2020, requiring cumulative impact assessments and meaningful community engagement before issuing permits.[296] In the South, states like North Carolina and Louisiana saw a surge in activism despite limited statutory frameworks. Groups such as the North Carolina Environmental Justice Network and the Louisiana Bucket Brigade used citizen science and air monitoring to collect real-time pollution data, which often served as evidence in legal complaints and public health studies.[297] Although Texas has lagged in statewide environmental justice policy and the Texas Commission on Environmental Quality has faced criticism for limited community engagement and lenient enforcement, local organizations such as the Port Arthur Community Action Network and Texas Environmental Justice Advocacy Services (t.e.j.a.s.) have taken the lead in holding industry accountable through public hearings, litigation, and grassroots data collection.[298] Their work underscores how local leadership can drive accountability, even in politically resistant environments.

Building on this community-driven model, several cities began formalizing environmental justice principles within their planning and zoning processes. At the municipal level, cities like Baltimore and Chicago have integrated EJ into planning and zoning. Baltimore's Office of Sustainability has embedded

EJ goals into its climate action plan and sustainability plan updates, aligning equity with land-use and housing strategies. Chicago established an Office of Environmental Equity and has advanced cumulative impact policies for industrial permitting, particularly in neighborhoods historically burdened by pollution and disinvestment. Other cities, including New York, Los Angeles, and Seattle, have launched resilience hubs and task forces to address urban heat, air pollution, and climate-related health disparities.[299] These local innovations reflect a growing recognition that environmental justice must be embedded in everyday governance and not treated as an afterthought.

Collaborations between community organizations and academic institutions have driven some of the most significant advances. Community-based participatory research empowers residents to codesign studies, collect data, and shape findings.[300] Schools such as Dillard University, Texas Southern University, and the University of Michigan have established research centers dedicated to environmental and climate justice, providing training, resources, and policy analysis to support community-led advocacy.[301] These partnerships help bridge the gap between technical expertise and community insight.

In 2007, a follow-up report titled *Toxic Wastes and Race at Twenty: 1987–2007* reaffirmed that even two decades later, race remained the most significant determinant of where hazardous waste facilities are located, with communities of color continuing to bear a disproportionate share of the burden.[302] Despite increased attention to EJ over a period of decades, environmental racism persists, underscoring the ongoing need for policy reform. When the original *Toxic Wastes and Race in the United States* report was released in 1987, researcher Charles Lee estimated that approximately fifteen million African Americans lived near uncontrolled toxic waste sites, including dumps, landfills, and Superfund locations.[303] More than thirty years later, that central finding remains disturbingly relevant. Race continues to be the most consistent predictor of exposure to environmental hazards in the United States.[304]

Recent analyses by the EPA confirm that Black, Latino, and Indigenous communities continue to face disproportionately high exposure to air pollutants, toxic waste, and industrial emissions compared to their White counterparts.[305] A 2021 study published in the *Proceedings of the National Academy of Sciences* found that people of color are exposed to 63% more air pollution than they generate through consumption, while White Americans encounter 17% *less* pollution than their consumption generates.[306] This imbalance reflects not only historic zoning decisions and industrial siting patterns, but also ongoing disparities in housing, infrastructure, and political influence. The unequal distribution of environmental burdens manifests in severe illnesses, a direct outcome of long-standing systemic neglect. Decades of policy promises have failed to dismantle these inequities, leaving residents to navigate daily exposure that would be considered unacceptable elsewhere. These findings reinforce what EJ advocates have long argued, that the right to clean air and water remains unequally protected in America, and true reform requires more than recognition; it demands accountability and structural change.

Climate change further magnifies these injustices. The same communities historically exposed to industrial toxins are now among the most vulnerable to flooding, heat waves, and extreme weather events. Hurricanes Katrina and Harvey revealed how environmental racism intersects with disaster vulnerability, where infrastructure neglect and historical segregation compound the effects of natural hazards.[307] Environmental justice is no longer just about pollution; it's about survival.

Recognizing this growing intersection between climate and equity, the Biden administration established the White House Environmental Justice Advisory Council (WHEJAC) and launched the Justice40 Initiative in 2021, marking a significant step toward embedding equity in federal investment.[308] Justice40 sought to direct 40% of the overall benefits of federal climate and clean energy funding to disadvantaged communities, addressing long-standing inequities in public investment. While ambitious, its success depended on transparency, community input, and a commitment from political leadership. Yet these initiatives faced persistent and political obstacles. Their implementation hinged on accurate data, interagency coordination, and durable institutional support. Without statutory authority, executive actions are subjected to weakening or reversal by future administrations. The Trump administration, for instance, demonstrated this vulnerability by scaling back EJ infrastructure, reducing advisory council activity, and deprioritizing EJ considerations across federal agencies. Moreover, communities continue to struggle with limited access to the resources and technical expertise required to navigate complex grant systems or permit reviews. For many, the process remains unclear and inaccessible.

In 2022, the EPA established the Office of Environmental Justice and External Civil Rights, merging civil rights enforcement with environmental protection.[309] This integration represents a long-awaited structural acknowledgment of what activists like Dr. Robert Bullard and Dr. Beverly Wright have argued for decades, that environmental justice is civil rights by another name. It's a recognition that pollution and discrimination often share the same zip code. True progress also requires confronting the political dimensions of environmental inequality. Regulatory agencies cannot remain neutral arbiters in the face of injustice. As Dr. Bullard has signaled, if a community is invisible, so are its problems. Making these communities visible through data, advocacy, and representation, remains the movement's most enduring challenge and greatest opportunity. Visibility is the first step toward accountability.

Ultimately, the progress since 1987 shows how far the movement has come and how far it still has to go. Real progress will depend on institutions having the courage, and communities having the power, to confront and dismantle the structures that have long normalized inequality. The challenge is to prevent future harm, and to repair the damages of the past. As the environmental justice movement enters its fifth decade, its mission endures. Its purpose is to ensure that no community is considered expendable and that clean air, safe water, and healthy environments are treated not as privileges, but as fundamental human rights. This is not just a policy goal; it is a moral obligation.

CHAPTER NINE

The Evolution of the EJ Movement

"While recent years have brought setbacks and persistent disparities, environmental justice is entering a new era—one defined by innovation, intersectional alliances, and a generation unwilling to accept the status quo."[310]

~ **Catherine Coleman Flowers**

Environmental and Climate Justice Advocate;

Founder and Director of the Center for Rural Enterprise and Environmental Justice

WITH OVER FOUR DECADES of research and activism, the environmental justice movement has become an integral part of the national and global dialogue on inequality, health, and sustainability.[311] What began as a set of community protests in the late 1970s has matured into a complex network of advocacy, science, law, and education. Weathering political resistance and institutional neglect, generations of activists have built a movement defined by resilience and inclusivity, forging alliances that cross race, class, and geography. Its reach now extends from small-town struggles over waste sites to international campaigns for climate and human rights, showing that environmental protection and social equity are inseparable goals.[312]

From its inception, the movement has understood that environmental harm does not occur in isolation. The same communities historically denied civil rights have also been denied clean air and water, safe housing, and healthy workplaces. These intersections between civil rights, public health, and environmental protection have long shaped the movement's strategies and definitions of justice.[313] What distinguishes environmental justice from earlier environmentalism is its insistence that people—not wilderness or wildlife alone—must be at the center of environmental policy. For communities living in the shadows of refineries, waste dumps, and power plants, the right to a healthy environment is not abstract; it is a necessity to live, breathe, and thrive without fear of poisoning.

As the EJ movement evolved, it became increasingly sophisticated in its use of data and technology. In the past, residents relied on anecdotal evidence and protest to gain attention; today, they use geographic information systems (GIS), remote sensing, and open-source mapping to document disparities with scientific precision.[314] Citizen scientists in overburdened communities now monitor air and water quality, track industrial emissions, and produce datasets that stand alongside those of governmental agencies. These tools not only expose patterns of harm but also provide leverage for litigation and policy reform. When communities can visualize their exposure—see it mapped, measured, and verified—they gain a powerful form of evidence that compels public responsibility.

Access to environmental data is more than a technical achievement; it represents a redistribution of power. The ability to collect and interpret information has historically been monopolized by agencies and corporations. By making data accessible to all, individuals and communities reclaim the right to define their own realities. This shift has allowed community-driven research projects to challenge state and corporate narratives, leading to new forms of "citizen evidence" that support lawsuits, zoning appeals, and health interventions.[315] These innovations underscore a key principle of the movement. Knowledge is power, and when communities control knowledge, they control their destinies.

Parallel to this technological evolution was the rise of a new era of coalition building. Scholars, faith leaders, and neighborhood organizers recognized that no single field could address environmental injustice alone. Public health experts partnered with housing advocates, lawyers collaborated with community groups, and educators worked alongside residents to translate research into policy. This interdisciplinary approach reflected the understanding that injustice operates across systems and must be confronted through equally interconnected solutions.

Legal advocacy became one of the movement's most visible arenas for change. Early cases like *Bean v. Southwestern Waste Management Corp.* (1979) demonstrated how civil rights law could be used to challenge discriminatory siting of hazardous facilities. Although plaintiffs often faced daunting evidentiary burdens, these cases created the foundation for environmental justice litigation.[316] In subsequent decades, nonprofit legal organizations such as Earthjustice and the Southern Environmental Law Center refined these strategies, using environmental statutes alongside civil rights frameworks to compel enforcement and accountability. Even when lawsuits failed to deliver sweeping victories, they forced recognition of systemic inequities and set precedents for stronger oversight.

The rise of EJ education marked another transformative phase. What began as a grassroots movement gradually entered universities, reshaping curricula and research agendas. Dr. Bunyan Bryant and Dr. Paul Mohai established one of the first academic environmental justice programs in the U.S. at the University of Michigan in 1992, creating a model that has since been replicated nationwide.[317] Their work underscored the importance of training future leaders who could navigate both community realities and institutional systems. EJ programs combine conflict resolution, sociology, geography, law, and public health, producing graduates equipped to conduct rigorous research while engaging directly with affected communities.

Equally influential has been the development of community-based participatory research (CBPR), a methodology that bridges the divide between scholars and residents.[318] In CBPR, communities codesign studies, collect data, and interpret results alongside researchers, ensuring that findings reflect lived experience and practical needs. This approach democratizes science by recognizing community members as co-researchers rather than passive subjects. The work of Dr. Sacoby Wilson at the University of Maryland exemplifies this model, linking public health research to environmental advocacy through partnerships that empower residents to monitor pollution and demand intervention.[319]

Such community–academic collaborations have had tangible policy impacts. Data generated through CBPR has informed environmental health regulations, influenced zoning reforms, and strengthened community grant applications. More importantly, it has shifted the culture of research itself, grounding academic inquiry in principles of reciprocity, respect, and relevance. In this way, the movement has redefined what constitutes legitimate expertise. Lived experience, once dismissed as "anecdotal," now stands alongside professional credential as a vital source of knowledge.

Philanthropy has also played an evolving role in sustaining the movement. For decades, environmental justice organizations struggled with chronic underfunding, often competing with larger, mainstream environmental groups for limited resources. In recent years, however, many philanthropic institutions have begun to adopt equity-based grantmaking practices that prioritize frontline leadership. Participatory and pooled funding models now invite community representatives to set priorities and decide where resources should flow.[320] In placing decision-making power in the hands of those most affected, these models reflect a philosophical shift from charity to solidarity.

Youth leadership has become one of the movement's most dynamic forces. A generation raised amid climate crisis and social activism has transformed the tools of advocacy. Through social media, podcasts, and digital storytelling, young organizers amplify local struggles to global audiences. They use platforms like Instagram and TikTok not only to share information but to humanize statistics through art and personal testimony.[321] For many, activism is as much about narrative as protest; it is about controlling representation in a digital landscape saturated with misinformation. These creative interventions have reenergized the movement, expanding its reach and accessibility to new audiences.

Social media's power lies in its immediacy. It allows communities to document and broadcast environmental harm in real time, bypassing traditional media filters. Viral videos of pollution spills, protests, or policy hearings can ignite national conversations within hours. Yet the speed of digital activism also carries risks. Without sustained engagement, online momentum can fade as quickly as it arises. Movement leaders caution that while technology amplifies voices, it cannot substitute for the patient work of organizing, coalition building, and education.[322] True transformation still happens in the slow, deliberate building of trust.

Storytelling, whether through digital platforms or community oral histories, remains central to environmental justice. The power of narrative lies in its capacity to make the invisible visible. A map can reveal where pollution occurs, but a story reveals what that pollution feels like. When combined with data, stories give moral weight to scientific findings, transforming policy debates into human imperatives. Documentaries, art exhibits, and personal essays have all contributed to reframing environmental justice as a moral and cultural issue as much as a political one.[323]

The movement's global dimension has expanded dramatically since the early 2000s. Environmental injustice is not confined to national borders; it is bound to transnational systems of extraction, trade, and consumption. U.S.-based activists have increasingly linked domestic struggles with international campaigns for climate and economic justice. Networks connecting communities in the Global South and North share strategies for legal reform, renewable energy, and sustainable development.[324] These partnerships recognize that the same corporate and economic structures that exploit vulnerable regions abroad also marginalize low-income and minority populations at home. The global solidarity forged through these alliances underscores that environmental justice is, at its core, a struggle for human rights.

Within this expanding global framework, the concept of "regenerative justice" has gained prominence. Building on the principles of restorative justice, it calls not merely for repairing harm but for creating conditions that sustain life and community resilience.[325] Regenerative justice integrates ecological restoration with social healing. This includes reclaiming brownfields for urban gardens, transforming polluted spaces into renewable energy sites, and prioritizing community ownership in redevelopment. It reframes justice as a living practice rather than a legal endpoint, envisioning a future in which healing replaces extraction and shared stewardship replaces exploitation.

Education, mutual aid, and legal advocacy together sustain the movement's long-term vitality. Universities train new researchers and organizers; communities teach one another through workshops, health fairs, and storytelling circles; and mutual aid networks provide immediate support when disaster strikes.[326] These systems of care exemplify a broader ethic of interdependence. When hurricanes devastate Gulf Coast towns or wildfires displace Western communities, it is often local networks, not distant agencies, that provide the first response. Environmental justice, in this sense, is as much about survival as it is about reform.

Legal innovation remains essential to this endurance. Despite restrictive precedents like *Alexander v. Sandoval* (2001), which limited the use of Title VI in civil rights claims, advocates continue to press new legal theories linking environmental harm to constitutional and human rights violations.[327] Some have argued that access to a safe environment should be recognized as a fundamental right protected under the Fourteenth Amendment's guarantees of life and liberty. Others draw on international human rights law to hold governments accountable for failing to protect vulnerable populations. These evolving strategies reflect a legal imagination shaped by the movement's moral conviction that environmental harm is a form of violence, and therefore justice must be both corrective and preventive.

Cultural change, however, remains the most enduring marker of progress. Through decades of steadfastness, environmental justice has shifted public consciousness about who counts as an environmentalist and what counts as an environmental issue.[328] Pollution, zoning, and infrastructure, once seen as technical or local concerns, are now recognized as matters of equity and civil rights. This redefinition is perhaps the movement's greatest achievement; it has expanded the moral vocabulary of justice itself.

Looking forward, the environmental justice movement's strength lies in its victories as well as in its adaptability. It continues to evolve, absorbing new ideas, technologies, and voices while remaining anchored in its founding principle that all people have the right to live free from environmental harm. Each generation inherits both the progress and the unfinished work of those before it. The struggle endures not because it has failed, but because those who benefit from environmental injustice continue to protect it.

As history shows, justice is not achieved by policy alone but by people who refuse to accept inequity as inevitable. The environmental justice movement reminds us that progress is cumulative, built through small victories, enduring coalitions, and unwavering commitment. It is a living testament to collective resilience. It is a reminder that even in the face of adversity, communities possess the power to reimagine and rebuild their futures. The work of environmental justice, in all its forms, remains one of the most urgent and transformative pursuits of our time.

CHAPTER TEN

Awareness to Action

"Get in good trouble, necessary trouble, and help redeem the soul of America."[329]

~ **John Lewis (1940–2020)**

American Civil Rights Leader

Former Chair of the Student Nonviolent Coordinating Committee (SNCC); Architect of the Selma Voting Rights Marches; Former U.S. Representative for Georgia's Fifth Congressional District (1987–2020)

THE ENVIRONMENTAL JUSTICE MOVEMENT did not emerge overnight. It grew out of generations of resistance, organizing, and advocacy by people who refused to accept inequality as normal. Rooted in the lived experiences of communities of color placed in harm's way, it stands at the intersection of civil rights, environmental protection, and public health. It is a cause defined not only by the fight for cleaner air and water, but by the demand to be seen, heard, and protected by the very laws that claim to serve all.

Long before environmental racism became part of public discourse, Black communities, Indigenous nations, and farmworker organizations were confronting pollution, toxic dumping, and unsafe working conditions. Civil rights leaders—such as Dr.

Martin Luther King Jr. and the Reverend James Lawson, who in 1968 supported sanitation workers in Memphis protesting dangerous labor conditions, and César Chávez and Dolores Huerta, who organized farmworkers against pesticide exposure—understood that environmental health was inseparable from human rights.[330] These early struggles laid the foundation for what would later become a national, and now global, movement for environmental equity.

Furthermore, the groundwork laid by early EJ advocates such as Dr. Robert Bullard, Dr. Beverly Wright, and Dr. Benjamin Chavis provided the foundation upon which the modern EJ movement would grow. Their work inspired a wave of local, national, and international organizing that broadened the fight from specific incidents of environmental racism to systemic reform. As the movement matured, it diversified, bringing together public health experts, lawyers, educators, and neighborhood activists to confront injustice in all its forms. It became more than a field of study or activism, but a unifying vision for social transformation.[331] As its coalition grew, so too did its vision. It became a demand for environmental protection that valued not just wilderness and wildlife, but also the people forced to live in the shadow of industry.

Over time, this fight for environmental equity evolved into a broad, intersectional initiative that now encompasses climate justice, water equity, food sovereignty, and disaster recovery. In the United States, leaders such as Dr. Dorceta Taylor, Dr. Mona Hanna-Attisha, Catherine Coleman Flowers, Dr. Beverly Wright, and Dr. Mustafa Santiago Ali have advanced the national conversation linking environmental racism to public health, poverty, and policy reform.[332] Globally, figures such as Dr. Wangari Maathai, founder of Kenya's Green Belt Movement and Nobel Peace Prize laureate, extended these principles across borders, demonstrating that these efforts transcend nations and are fundamentally a human rights struggle.[333] Their collective work underscores that the pursuit for justice is not confined to one issue; it is a comprehensive demand for dignity, safety, and sustainability across every sphere of life.

Today, the push for reform remains one of the most urgent and transformative movements of our time. Federal initiatives such as the White House Environmental Justice Advisory Council and the Justice40 Initiative, launched under the Biden administration, once signaled unprecedented progress toward embedding equity into federal policy. Yet under the Trump administration that followed, many of these efforts were rolled back, defunded, or placed under review, reminding us how fragile progress can be when it relies solely on political will.[334] As federal commitments waver, the work needs to continue from the ground up. It begins in neighborhoods where residents organize to stop refinery expansions, test their own water, or demand fair housing free from industrial contamination; it grows in classrooms where students learn to map pollution in their own communities; and it gains strength through coalitions that connect local struggles to national and global campaigns, ensuring that the call for justice cannot be silenced by policy reversals.

This powerful legacy of resistance teaches that progress is not achieved by policy alone, but by people, ordinary individuals who decide that the status quo is unacceptable. The power of this movement lies in its inclusivity. You do not need a title, degree, or position to contribute. You only need awareness, empathy, and commitment. Each action, no matter how small, contributes to the larger fight for a fair and sustainable future.

To advance this cause, anyone motivated to make a difference can take tangible steps to become part of the solution. Start by learning about the organizations and initiatives working in your region. Engage with community-based environmental groups, many of which welcome volunteers for everything from neighborhood cleanups to public hearings. Support or join national advocacy networks such as the NAACP Environmental and Climate Justice Program, GreenLatinos, WE ACT for Environmental Justice, the Indigenous Environmental Network, and Earthjustice.[335] These organizations operate at the intersection of science, law, and community organizing, mobilizing data, policy, and people to advance equity and protection.

Local involvement remains the foundation of change. Attend city council meetings where zoning and permitting decisions are made. Speak up for policies that promote cleaner energy, equitable transit, and public health protections. Collaborate with educators to bring environmental literacy into schools. Advocate for inclusive decision-making that ensures residents have a seat at the table when environmental and land-use choices are made. Remember that collective advocacy, whether through petitions, partnerships, or public comment, can transform community concerns into actionable reform.

The architects of the EJ movement have offered insights that remain essential. Listen first to those most affected, document conditions through credible research, and press on even when progress feels slow. Environmental justice work requires patience, empathy, and a belief that equity is achievable. The task before us is to make disenfranchised communities and their struggles visible, and to translate visibility into accountability.

This book was written not only to chronicle injustice but to awaken participation. The movement for environmental justice is still being written, one action at a time. Whether you are a policymaker, educator, student, or concerned neighbor, your engagement matters. The call to action is both local and universal. Protect the places you love, uplift the people who are unheard, and insist that environmental protection is a right, not a privilege. Becoming part of a grassroots environmental justice group is one of the most powerful ways to channel conviction into impact. The following section provides a practical, step-by-step guide to help you connect, organize, and advocate effectively within your own community.

Identify Local Groups Aligned with Your Interests

- Research grassroots EJ organizations in your area through online searches and community bulletin boards, and attend local events or meetings to understand each group's mission, culture, and activities.

- Seek groups that focus on issues you care about, such as pollution, land use, climate justice, or community health.

Reach Out and Begin Actively Participating

- After contacting a local group, clearly communicate your interests, skills, and availability. Ask about the organization's goals, membership process, and ways new members can contribute.

- Begin to build relationships with neighbors and local leaders by staying informed and regularly attending meetings. Engage in discussions to broaden your understanding and perspective.

- As your involvement deepens over time, volunteer to steer committees, organize events, and oversee campaigns.

- Collaborate with fellow members and partner organizations, valuing the distinct strengths and perspectives each contributes. Engage actively in town halls, public forums, and rallies to strengthen alliances, amplify shared goals, and increase community visibility.

  - Building strong coalitions not only expands influence but also fosters knowledge exchange, capacity building, and resilience in the face of opposition from powerful interests. Well-organized partnerships have the power to shape policy and sustain lasting community empowerment.

- Foster an environment of mutual respect by actively listening to and honoring the knowledge and leadership of longtime frontline community members. Value diverse perspectives, especially from those most affected by environmental challenges. Create opportunities for these leaders to take part in decision-making and represent their communities in public forums, policy discussions, and coalition meetings.

Learn and Stay Informed

- Learn about local environmental justice challenges, relevant laws, and community history.

- Stay updated on policy developments.

- Commit to reading foundational and contemporary works on environmental justice and environmental racism. The following list highlights notable authors and their most influential works.

Authors and Writers	Key Works
Adrienne Maree Brown, social justice theorist and movement strategist	*Emergent Strategy: Shaping Change, Changing Worlds* (2017)
Beverly Wright, founder and executive director of the Deep South Center for Environmental Justice and professor of sociology at Dillard University	*The Wrong Complexion for Protection: How the Government Response to Disaster Endangers African American Communities* (coauthored by Robert Bullard, 2012)
Catherine Coleman Flowers, founder of the Center for Rural Enterprise and Environmental Justice	*Waste: One Woman's Fight Against America's Dirty Secret* (2020)

Dorceta Taylor, distinguished American environmental sociologist renowned for her groundbreaking work on EJ and racism, serves as the Wangari Maathai Professor of Environmental and Sustainability Studies at the Yale School of the Environment	*The Environment and the People in American Cities, 1600s–1900s: Disorder, Inequality, and Social Change* (2009) *Toxic Communities: Environmental Racism, Industrial Pollution, and Residential Mobility* (2014) *The Rise of the American Conservation Movement: Power, Privilege, and Environmental Protection* (2016)
Harriet Washington, award-winning writer, medical ethicist, and scholar	*A Terrible Thing to Waste: Environmental Racism and Its Assault on the American Mind* (2019)
Ingrid R. G. Waldron, Hope Chair in Peace and Health at McMaster University and founder of The ENRICH Project	*There's Something in the Water: Environmental Racism in Indigenous and Black Communities* (2018)
Isaias Hernandez, founder of an environmental website and educational platform that uses storytelling and multimedia content to bring intersectional EJ education to a broad audience	*Queer Brown Vegan* **Digital platform**
Laura Pulido, writer of numerous articles exploring Chicano environmental justice and economic disparities	*Struggles in the Southwest* (1996)

Luke W. Cole and Sheila R. Foster, authors of the foundational book tracing EJ legal struggles and grassroots movements	*From the Ground Up: Environmental Racism and the Rise of the Environmental Justice Movement* (2001)
Melissa Checker, urban anthropologist and professor of urban studies and environmental psychology at the City University of New York (CUNY) Graduate Center and Queens College	*Polluted Promises: Environmental Racism and the Search for Justice in a Southern Town* (2005)
Miya Yoshitani, former executive director of the Asian Pacific Environmental Network (APEN) and leading EJ advocate	"Tackling the Intersections of Poverty and Pollution in Asian and Pacific Islander Communities" (2016) **Policy report/essay**
Robert Bullard, American sociologist, distinguished professor at Texas Southern University and director of the Bullard Center for Environmental and Climate Justice, widely recognized as the father of environmental justice	*Dumping in Dixie: Race, Class, and Environmental Quality* (1990) *Unequal Protection: Environmental Justice and Communities of Color* (1996) *The Quest for Environmental Justice: Human Rights and the Politics of Pollution* (2005)
Winona LaDuke, Indigenous environmental activist and author	*All Our Relations: Native Struggles for Land and Life* (1999) *Recovering the Sacred: The Power of Naming and Claiming* (2005)

Advocate and Engage in Policy

- Contact local, state, and national representatives to push for stronger environmental protections and legislative change.

- Support petitions and campaigns that advocate for systemic change in communities affected by environmental injustice.

Leverage Social Media and Storytelling for Greater Impact

- Use social media as a tool for advocacy by raising awareness, amplifying community voices, and inspiring action through compelling, informative content.

- Use media platforms to elevate community concerns and solutions. Write blog posts to inform, submit op-eds to influence policy, and join podcasts to foster dialogue and inspire action.

Practice Economic Activism

- Organize or join peaceful protests against corporations with poor environmental track records.
    - Demonstrations are a powerful form of direct action that draw public attention to environmental injustice and hold corporations accountable for harmful practices. Effective protests often

combine on-the-ground participation with social media outreach to increase visibility and pressure decision-makers for change.

- Support businesses and organizations that demonstrate genuine environmental and social responsibility. Direct your consumer power toward companies with transparent sustainability practices and equitable community engagement.

Contribute Through Giving and Grant Participation

- Donate to legal funds that support environmental justice litigation.
    - Donating is a powerful way to sustain the fight for accountability. Your contribution will provide the financial resources necessary for communities and advocacy groups to challenge polluters, negligent corporations, and weak government enforcement. Successful lawsuits can result in policy reforms, cleanup mandates, compensation for damages, and stronger implementation of environmental laws. Supporting legal funds also helps sustain advocacy over the long term, making it one of the most strategic forms of civic engagement.
- Consider applying for grants that support community-driven projects aimed at advancing environmental

equity, building local capacity, and improving public health outcomes.

Join Forces with Local, National, and Global Organizations to Strengthen Your Reach

- The following list highlights reputable organizations and their areas of environmental focus.

Local	Environmental Justice Summary
Asian Pacific Environmental Network (APEN)	California-based grassroots organizing in Asian American and Pacific Islander communities for EJ
Center for Engagement, Environmental Justice and Health INpowering Communities (CEEJH INC)	Organization based in the mid-Atlantic empowering underserved and overburdened communities to tackle environmental injustice and health inequities
GreenLatinos	U.S.-based group bridging environmental and social justice with emphasis on Latino frontline communities
Harvard Law School, Environmental Justice Clinic	Provides legal training for students and litigates EJ cases with local and regional impacts
WE ACT for Environmental Justice	Landmark Harlem-based pioneers advancing EJ policy and community advocacy

National	
Center for Environmental Health	Reduces toxic exposure and seeks accountability for those living in vulnerable communities
Clean Water Action	Centers EJ in campaigns to protect safe drinking water for all communities
Climate Justice Alliance	National coalition of grassroots EJ groups
Earthjustice	Leading U.S. public interest law firm litigating for EJ and communities' right to clean air, clean water, and climate protections
Earthworks	Confronts and tackles extractive industries harming disproportionately affected frontline communities
Environmental Defense Fund (EDF)	U.S.-based advocacy organization integrating equity and EJ in climate and energy policy
Green America	Builds sustainable economy aligned and intersecting with EJ values and principles
National Wildlife Federation (EJ and Climate Adaptation Programs)	Promotes equitable, community-driven strategies to help vulnerable communities adapt to climate change
Natural Resources Defense Council (NRDC)	Major U.S. environmental law and advocacy organization embedding EJ in policy campaigns and legal battles
Sierra Club (EJ Program)	Conducts U.S.-wide grassroots campaigns centering on frontline communities in climate and energy fights
The Solutions Project	Funds and elevates frontline EJ-focused clean energy leadership

Union of Concerned Scientists	Uses science to advance climate justice and equitable policies
International	
350.org	Global grassroots climate justice organization
Amazon Watch	Supports Indigenous EJ struggles in the Amazon rainforest
Earth Action International	Advocacy network supporting environmental and social justice campaigns worldwide
Earth Day Network	Global education and mobilization with EJ as part of its justice-centered messaging
Earth Guardians	Global youth-led movement linking art, activism, and EJ
Earth Island Institute	Supports grassroots organizations and youth leaders globally, often advancing EJ directly
Ecojustice (Canada)	Environmental law group advancing EJ in Canada and beyond
Environmental Justice Foundation (U.K.)	Strong EJ mandate linking human rights and environmental protection in global campaigns
Environmental Law Alliance Worldwide (ELAW)	Global network of lawyers aiding EJ litigation
Franciscans International	Faith-based group advocating for EJ at the UN and global forums
Friends of the Earth International	Federation of grassroots organizations advancing EJ globally
Global Exchange	Works on international solidarity campaigns around EJ and social rights

Grassroots International	Global solidarity philanthropy organization funding frontline EJ and social movements across the Global South
Greenpeace	International network with strategic EJ campaigns confronting issues such as toxic waste and fossil fuels
World Resources Institute (WRI)	Research-driven global policy think tank integrating EJ into climate/equity frameworks

Environmental justice work is a long-term commitment that requires patience and persistence. Advocates are encouraged to embrace the journey both by celebrating small wins and learning from setbacks, recognizing that progress often comes in incremental steps rather than instant transformation. Sustained engagement builds the foundation for lasting change, as this collective effort grows stronger through consistency and shared perseverance.

Seasoned organizers and community leaders play a vital role in mentoring new participants, sharing knowledge, and cultivating leadership from within. By investing in others, you help ensure the vitality and continuity of this ongoing struggle, empowering fresh voices to carry the work forward.

At its heart, environmental justice is a shared responsibility that flourishes through dedication, collaboration, and the belief that a more equitable and sustainable future is both possible and worth fighting for. Each act of advocacy, each conversation, and each community victory adds to a larger legacy of resistance and renewal. The movement's strength lies not in a single leader or moment, but in the countless people who choose, day after day, to stand up for justice and protect the places we call home.

EPILOGUE

ENVIRONMENTAL JUSTICE IN AMERICA has always been more than a question of pollution; it is a reflection of who is protected and who is left behind. As the climate crisis accelerates, the same communities long burdened by industrial contamination now face compounding threats (rising seas, intensifying heat, and stronger storms) layered atop chronic toxic exposure. In places like Louisiana's Cancer Alley and Port Arthur, Texas, climate change is not a distant future but a daily multiplier of risk. The floods arrive faster, the recovery takes longer, and the financial losses run deeper for those already constrained by redlining's geographic inheritance and segregated infrastructure. Climate is the accelerant, and policy remains the match.

The science is clear. Climate change amplifies environmental inequity. Urban "heat islands" and floodplains line up with historic redlining maps; neighborhoods once segregated under Jim Crow often have fewer trees, more asphalt, and older, leak-prone housing. When extreme weather strikes, these same blocks shoulder outsized harm, not through "natural" selection, but through policy choice. COVID-19 made the pattern undeniable. Communities of color suffered higher mortality and morbidity tied to air pollution and environmental burden, a convergence of public health and environmental inequity that lingered beyond the pandemic.[336]

After 2020, a wave of government reforms tried to confront this history. The federal Justice40 commitment and related executive orders sought to steer at least 40% of certain federal investments to disadvantaged communities, standardize EJ screening tools, and embed equity across agencies.[337] But this scaffolding is now in flux. In early 2025, the Trump administration rescinded key Biden-era climate and EJ orders, which ended Justice40, the EJ Scorecard (a public dashboard tracking agencies' progress on EJ goals), and the Climate and Economic Justice Screening Tool (a mapping tool identifying disadvantaged communities for federal investment). That decision removed the clearest federal mechanism for channeling benefits to communities long overburdened by pollution.[338]

Two additional shifts define the present risk landscape. First, in June 2024 the Supreme Court overturned Chevron deference in *Loper Bright Enterprises v. Raimondo* (2024). Chevron had required courts to defer to agency interpretations of ambiguous statutes, and its reversal has made environmental policies, environmental justice protections, and climate regulations more vulnerable to legal challenges.[339] Second, since early 2025, several EPA policy proposals have signaled a shift toward regulatory flexibility rather than expansion of existing rules. Public announcements have emphasized reducing regulatory burdens, including reviews of greenhouse-gas standards for fossil-fuel power plants and potential revisions to federal vehicle-emissions programs. These moves have raised concerns among environmental justice advocates about shifting costs and risks back onto fence-line and low-income communities.[340] Independent analysts warn that these reversals will raise U.S.

power sector emissions for years, locking in higher cumulative pollution exposure for those already at risk.[341]

The pattern extends beyond rulemaking to governance itself. Enforcement capacity and public-participation safeguards, the core protections for EJ communities, are weakened when advisory panels are politicized, when the scope of environmental review under the National Environmental Policy Act (NEPA) is narrowed, or when agencies face sustained budget cuts and staff attrition. The compounded effect is simple. It means fewer inspections, fewer penalties, and slower responses, with the steepest consequences in the very zip codes that lack the wealth to buffer harm.[342]

If climate readiness becomes another arena where resilience is a privilege, then "green transition" risks repeating old hierarchies under a new name. Protecting the planet without protecting its most vulnerable inhabitants is a hollow victory. Environmental justice requires more than emissions targets; it requires institutional durability (so rules outlast administrations), procedural power (so communities can meaningfully shape decisions), and material investment (so benefits flow where harm has been historically concentrated). In practice, that means restoring and strengthening community-level screening tools and benefits tests, designing pollution standards that explicitly account for cumulative burden, and insulating public health science from political volatility.[343]

The struggle is unfinished, but the path is visible. Communities that endured centuries of dispossession have also engineered the most durable solutions. From parish-level organizing in Louisiana to citywide coalitions against heat and flooding, they are not merely the subjects of harm; they are the authors of resilience. What remains is a national decision about governance itself. The question is whether the United States will continue to treat environmental protection as optional, subject to deregulatory tides and legal crosswinds, or finally build a system where clean air, safe water, and climate security are nonnegotiable rights for all.

ENDNOTES

1. Fannie Lou Hamer, "Testimony Before the Credentials Committee at the Democratic National Convention, Atlantic City, New Jersey, August 22, 1964," in *The Speeches of Fannie Lou Hamer: To Tell It Like It Is*, eds. Maegan Parker Brooks and Davis W. Houck (University Press of Mississippi, 2011).

2. Bullard, Robert D. *Dumping in Dixie: Race, Class, and Environmental Quality*. 3rd ed. (Westview Press, 2000).

3. Robert D. Bullard et al., *Toxic Wastes and Race at Twenty: 1987–2007* (United Church of Christ Justice and Witness Ministries, 2007), 3, https://www.ucc.org/wp-content/uploads/2021/03/toxic-wastes-and-race-at-twenty-1987-2007.pdf.

4. Bullard et al., *Toxic Wastes and Race at Twenty*.

5. Michael Mascarenhas, "The Flint Water Crisis. A Case of Environmental Injustice or Environmental Racism" (2016) (Written Testimony Submitted to the Michigan Civil Rights Commission Hearings on the Flint Water Crisis), https://www.michigan.gov/-/media/Project/Websites/mdcr/public-comments/2016/mascarenhas_testimony.pdf.

6. Johan Galtung, "Violence, Peace, and Peace Research," *Journal of Peace Research* 6, no. 3 (1969).

7. Bullard, *Dumping in Dixie*.

8. United Church of Christ, Commission for Racial Justice, *Toxic Wastes and Race in the United States: A National Report on the Racial and Socio-Economic Characteristics of Communities with Hazardous Waste Sites* (United Church of Christ, 1987).

9. Bullard et al., *Toxic Wastes and Race at Twenty*.

10. Bullard, *Dumping in Dixie*.

11. Ibid.

12. Beverly Wright, "The Geography of Risk: Environmental Justice in the South," in *Race, Place, and Environmental Justice after Hurricane Katrina: Struggles to Reclaim, Rebuild, and Revitalize New Orleans and the Gulf Coast*, eds. Robert D. Bullard and Beverly Wright. Westview Press, 2009.

13. Ijeoma Oluo (@ijeomaoluo), Twitter, July 14, 2019, https://twitter.com/IjeomaOluo/status/1150565193832943617 (link no longer valid).

14. Robert D. Bullard, remarks at the 11th Annual Environmental Justice & Health Disparities Symposium, sponsored by the Center for Engagement, Environmental Justice & Health (CEEJH), September 10–13, 2024.

15. Martin Luther King Jr., "I Have a Dream," speech delivered at the March on Washington for Jobs and Freedom, August 28, 1963, Washington, D.C., in *A Testament of Hope: The Essential Writings and Speeches of Martin Luther King, Jr.*, ed. James M. Washington (HarperCollins, 1986).

16. Bullard, *Dumping in Dixie*.

17. Robert D. Bullard, "Anatomy of Environmental Racism and the Environmental Justice Movement," in *Confronting Environmental Racism: Voices from the Grassroots*, ed. Robert D. Bullard. South End Press, 1993.

18. Maudlyne Ihejirika, "What Is Environmental Racism?" Natural Resources Defense Council, February 24, 2023, https://www.nrdc.org/stories/what-environmental-racism.

19. Bullard, *Dumping in Dixie*; Steve Lerner, *Sacrifice Zones: The Front Lines of Toxic Chemical Exposure in the United States* (MIT Press, 2010).

20. Galtung, "Violence, Peace, and Peace Research"; Bullard, *Dumping in Dixie*; Paul Farmer, *Pathologies of Power: Health, Human Rights, and the New War on the Poor* (University of California Press, 2003).

21. Harriet A. Washington, *A Terrible Thing to Waste: Environmental Racism and Its Assault on the American Mind* (Little, Brown Spark, 2019), 167; Ellen Griffith Spears, *Baptized in PCBs: Race, Pollution, and Justice in an All-American Town* (University of North Carolina Press, 2014).

22. Robert D. Bullard and Beverly Wright, *The Wrong Complexion for Protection: How the Government Response to Disaster Endangers African American Communities* (New York University Press, 2012).

23. Lylla Younes et al., "Poison in the Air," *ProPublica*, November 14, 2019, accessed November 2, 2025, https://www.propublica.org/article/toxmap-poison-in-the-air.

24. Spears, *Baptized in PCBs*; Bullard and Wright, *The Wrong Complexion for Protection*.

25. Bullard, *Dumping in Dixie*.

26. Oladele A. Ogunseitan, "Environmental Racism," *Salem Press Encyclopedia* (2019).

27. Robert W. Collin, "Environmental Equity and the Need for Government Intervention: Two Proposals," *Environment* 35, no. 9 (1993): 41–45.

28. Collin, "Environmental Equity."

29. Civil Rights Act of 1964, 42 U.S.C. § 2000d; Bullard, *Dumping in Dixie*.

30. Bullard, *Dumping in Dixie*.

31. Ibid.

32. *Warren County v. State of North Carolina*, 528 F. Supp. 276 (E.D.N.C. 1981).

33. Bullard, *Dumping in Dixie*.

34. Ibid.

35. "The Origins of EPA," U.S. Environmental Protection Agency, last updated November 6, 2025, https://www.epa.gov/history/origins-epa.

36. Bullard, *Dumping in Dixie*.

37. Ibid.

38. Ibid.

39. Dorceta E. Taylor, *Toxic Communities: Environmental Racism, Industrial Pollution, and Residential Mobility* (NYU Press, 2014).

40. U.S. General Accounting Office, *Siting of Hazardous Waste Landfills and Their Correlation with Racial and Economic Status of Surrounding Communities* (U.S. General Accounting Office, 1983).

41. United Church of Christ, *Toxic Wastes and Race in the United States*.

42. Ibid.

43. Ibid.

44. Ibid.

45. Robert D. Bullard, interview by *Journal of International Affairs*, "Addressing Environmental Racism," *Columbia SIPA Journal of International*

Affairs, February 11, 2020, https://jia.sipa.columbia.edu/news/addressing-environmental-racism.

46. Laura Pulido, "Rethinking Environmental Racism: White Privilege and Urban Development in Southern California," *Annals of the Association of American Geographers* 90, no. 1 (2000).

47. Bullard, *Dumping in Dixie*.

48. Ibid.

49. Liam Downey and Brian Hawkins, "Race, Income, and Environmental Inequality in the United States," *Sociological Perspectives* 51, no. 4 (2008).

50. Robert D. Bullard, "Environmental Justice in the 21st Century: Race Still Matters," *Phylon* 49, no. 3/4 (2001).

51. Bullard, *Dumping in Dixie*.

52. Jaap J. Vos, Alka Sapat, and Khi V. Thai, "Blaming the Victim: The Role of Decision-Makers in the Occurrence of Environmental Injustice." *International Journal of Public Administration* 25, no. 2/3 (2002).

53. Taylor, *Toxic Communities*.

54. U.S. Environmental Protection Agency, *Office of Environmental Justice in Action*, fact sheet, September 2017, https://www.epa.gov/sites/default/files/2017-09/documents/epa_office_of_environmental_justice_factsheet.pdf.

55. U.S. Commission on Civil Rights, *Environmental Justice: Examining the Environmental Protection Agency's Compliance and Enforcement of Title VI and Executive Order 12,898*. U.S. Commission on Civil Rights, 2016.

56. U.S. Commission on Civil Rights, *Environmental Justice*.

57. Robert D. Bullard and Beverly Wright, *Race, Place, and Environmental Justice After Hurricane Katrina* (Westview Press, 2009).

58. Dorceta E. Taylor, *The Environment and the People in American Cities, 1600s–1900s: Disorder, Inequality, and Social Change* (Duke University Press, 2009).

59. Robert D. Bullard, ed., *The Quest for Environmental Justice: Human Rights and the Politics of Pollution* (Sierra Club Books, 2005), xxiii–xxv.

60. Nikole Hannah-Jones, interview by Ali Velshi, *Velshi*, MSNBC, February 2, 2025, https://youtu.be/0rUk1FNe7ac.

61. Cara Steinberg, "Visualizing Environmental Injustice with Interactive Data: Cancer Alley, Louisiana," *FracTracker* Alliance, December 31, 2024, https://www.fractracker.org/2024/12/visualizing-environmental-injustice-with-interactive-data-cancer-alley-louisiana/.

62. Steinberg, "Visualizing Environmental Injustice."

63. Ibid.

64. United Nations, "Environmental Racism in Louisiana's 'Cancer Alley' Must End, Say UN Human Rights Experts," *UN News*, March 2, 2021, https://news.un.org/en/story/2021/03/1086172.

65. Zoe Friese, "Fight or Flight: A Story of Survival and Justice in Cancer Alley," *Women Leading Change: Case Studies on Women, Gender, and Feminism* 7, no. 2 (2023). https://journals.tulane.edu/ncs/article/download/3789/3557.

66. Friese, "Fight or Flight."

67. Courtney J. Keehan, "Lessons from Cancer Alley: How the Clean Air Act Has Failed to Protect Public Health in Southern Louisiana," *Colorado Environmental Law Journal* 29, no. 2 (2022). https://celj.cu.law/?p=696.

68. Friese, "Fight or Flight."

69. "Environmental Racism in Louisiana," University Network for Human Rights, updated February 2021, https://www.humanrightsnetwork.org/projects/cancer-alley.

70. Ibid.

71. Ibid.

72. Susan D. Carle, Reconstruction's Lessons, Columbia Journal of Race and Law 13 (2023): 734, https://digitalcommons.wcl.american.edu/facsch_lawrev/2212.

73. "Environmental Racism in Louisiana," University Network for Human Rights.

74. Byne F. Goodman, *The Black Codes, 1865–1867* (bachelor's thesis, University of Illinois, 1912), https://archive.org/details/blackcodes18651800good; John K. Bardes, "Redefining Vagrancy: Policing Freedom and Disorder in Reconstruction New Orleans, 1862–1868," *Journal of Southern History* 83, no. 2 (2017). https://www.jstor.org/stable/44784137.

75. Nakia D. Parker, "Black Codes and Slave Codes," *Oxford Bibliographies in African American Studies*, last modified March 25, 2020, https://www.oxfordbibliographies.com/abstract/document/obo-9780190280024/obo-9780190280024-0083.xml; Bardes, "Redefining Vagrancy."

76. Laurence W. Mazzeno, "Analysis: Louisiana Black Code," *EBSCO Research Starters*, 2021, https://www.ebsco.com/research-starters/history/analysis-louisiana-black-code.

77. "The Southern 'Black Codes' of 1865–66," Teach Democracy, accessed November 18, 2025, https://teachdemocracy.org/online-lesson/the-southern-black-codes-of-1865-66/.

78. Matthew J. Mancini, "Convict Leasing," *64 Parishes*, May 27, 2011, https://64parishes.org/entry/convict-leasing.

79. Nathan Cardon, "Less Than Mayhem: Louisiana's Convict Lease, 1865–1901," *Louisiana History: The Journal of the Louisiana Historical Association* 58, no.4 (2017), https://www.jstor.org/stable/26290931.

80. W.E.B. Du Bois, Black Reconstruction in America, 1860–1880 (New York: Harcourt, Brace and Company, 1935).

81. Mazzeno, Laurence W. 2025. "Analysis: Louisiana Black Code." *Research Starters: History*. EBSCO Information Services. Accessed December 2, 2025. https://www.ebsco.com/research-starters/history/analysis-louisiana-black-code.

82. Warren Hoffnagle, "The Southern Homestead Act: Its Origins and Operation," *The Historian* 32, no. 4 (1970). https://www.jstor.org/stable/pdf/24441013.pdf.

83. Evelyn Hartwell, "The Impact of Jim Crow Laws on Modern Racial Inequality," blacklivesmatteratschool.org, April 23, 2025, https://blacklivesmatteratschool.org/the-impact-of-jim-crow-laws-on-modern-racial-inequality/.

84. Lukas Althoff and Hugo Reichardt, "Jim Crow and Black Economic Progress after Slavery," *Quarterly Journal of Economics* 139, no. 4 (2024). https://doi.org/10.1093/qje/qjae023.

85. Julian Johnson, "The System That Destroyed Black Wealth: How Jim Crow Erased Generations of Black Landowners," Julian Johnson Law, April 14, 2025, https://julianjohnsonlaw.com/the-system-that-destroyed-black-wealth-how-jim-crow-erased-generations-of-black-landowners/.

86. Robert D. Bullard, "The Legacy of American Apartheid and Environmental Racism," *Journal of Civil Rights and Economic Development* 9, no. 2 (1994). https://scholarship.law.stjohns.edu/jcred/vol9/iss2/3/.

87. Thomas J. Sugrue, *The Origins of the Urban Crisis: Race and Inequality in Postwar Detroit*. Princeton University Press, 1996.

88. David R. Williams and Chiquita Collins, "Racial Residential Segregation: A Fundamental Cause of Racial Disparities in Health," *Public Health Reports* 116, no. 5 (2001). https://pmc.ncbi.nlm.nih.gov/articles/PMC1497358/pdf/12042604.pdf.

89. David R. Williams, "How Racism Makes Us Sick," TED Talk, Palm Springs, CA, November 2016, 17 min., 18 sec., https://www.ted.com/talks/david_r_williams_how_racism_makes_us_sick.

90. Williams, "How Racism Makes Us Sick."

91. Williams and Collins, "Racial Residential Segregation."

92. Douglas S. Massey and Nancy A. Denton, *American Apartheid: Segregation and the Making of the Underclass*. Harvard University Press, 1993.

93. Massey and Denton, *American Apartheid*.

94. Nikole Hannah-Jones, *The 1619 Project: A New Origin Story*. One World, 2021.

95. Hannah-Jones, *The 1619 Project*.

96. Keeanga-Yamahtta Taylor, *Race for Profit: How Banks and the Real Estate Industry Undermined Black Homeownership*. University of North Carolina Press, 2019.

97. Bruce Mitchell and Juan Franco, "HOLC 'Redlining' Maps: The Persistent Structure of Segregation and Economic Inequality," *National Community Reinvestment Coalition*, March 20, 2018, https://ncrc.org/holc/.

98. Ibid.

99. Ibid.

100. Taylor, *Race for Profit*.

101. Bullard, "The Legacy of American Apartheid."

102. Bullard, "The Legacy of American Apartheid."

103. Ibid.

104. Junia Howell and James R. Elliott, "Damages Done: The Longitudinal Impacts of Natural Hazards on Wealth Inequality in the United States," *Social Problems* 66, no. 3 (2019): 448–467, https://www.jstor.org/stable/26991002.

105. Howell and Ellitt, "Damages Done."

106. Ibid.

107. Ibid.

108. Ibid.

109. Exec. Order No. 12898, "Federal Actions to Address Environmental Justice in Minority Populations and Low-Income Populations," *Federal Register* 59, no. 32 (February 16, 1994), https://www.archives.gov/files/federal-register/executive-orders/pdf/12898.pdf.

110. Exec. Order No. 12898.

111. Julia Mizutani, "In the Backyard of Segregated Neighborhoods: An Environmental Justice Case Study of Louisiana," *Georgetown Environmental Law Review* 31 (2019). https://www.law.georgetown.edu/environmental-law-review/wp-content/uploads/sites/18/2019/04/GT-GELR190004.pdf.

112. Mizutani, "In the Backyard of Segregated Neighborhoods."

113. Ibid.

114. R. W. Collin, "Environmental Equity and the Need for Government Intervention: Two Proposals," *Environment* 35, no. 9 (1993); Bullard, *Dumping in Dixie*.

115. Ibid.

116. Bullard, *Dumping in Dixie*; Bullard, Robert D. 2001. "Environmental Justice in the 21st Century: Race Still Matters." Phylon 49 (3/4). https://doi.org/10.2307/3132626.

117. Bullard, "Environmental Justice in the 21st Century."

118. Ana Isabel Baptista et al., *Local Policies for Environmental Justice: A National Scan*. Tishman Environment and Design Center at The New School, 2019. https://www.nrdc.org/sites/default/files/local-policies-environmental-justice-national-scan-tishman-201902.pdf.

119. Baptista et al., *Local Policies*.

120. Ibid.

121. Center for Constitutional Rights, "Landmark Environmental Racism Case: Cancer Alley Residents Argue in Court for Moratorium on Toxic Plants in Black Districts," press release, October 7, 2024, https://ccrjustice.org/

home/press-center/press-releases/landmark-environmental-racism-case-cancer-alley-residents-argue.

122. Center for Constitutional Rights, "Landmark Environmental Racism Case."

123. Ibid.

124. Galtung, "Violence, Peace, and Peace Research."

125. Yves Winter, "Violence and Visibility," *New Political Science* 34, no. 2 (2012).

126. Elizabeth Lewis, "What Is Structural Violence? Anthropological Definition and Examples," *ThoughtCo*, last updated May 4, 2025, https://www.thoughtco.com/structural-violence-4174956.

127. Johan Galtung, "Twenty-Five Years of Peace Research: Ten Challenges and Some Responses," *Journal of Peace Research* 22, no. 2 (1985).

128. Andrew Dilts, "Revisiting Johan Galtung's Concept of Structural Violence," *New Political Science* 2 (2012).

129. Daniel J. Christie, "Reducing Direct and Structural Violence: The Human Needs Theory," *Peace & Conflict: Journal of Peace Psychology* 3, no. 4 (1997).

130. Taylor, *Toxic Communities*.

131. Ibid.

132. Bullard, *Dumping in Dixie*.

133. Dennis J. D. Sandole, "Extending the Reach of Basic Human Needs," in *Conflict Resolution and Human Needs: Linking Theory and Practice*, eds. Kevin Avruch and Christopher Mitchell. Routledge, 2013.

134. Derrick Bell, *Faces at the Bottom of the Well: The Permanence of Racism*. Basic Books, 1992.

135. Bell, *Faces at the Bottom of the Well*.

136. Derrick Bell, *Silent Covenants: Brown v. Board of Education and the Unfulfilled Hopes for Racial Reform*. Oxford University Press, 2004.

137. Bell, *Silent Covenants*.

138. Ibid.

139. Dilts, "Revisiting Johan Galtung's Concept of Structural Violence."

140. Vos, Sapat, and Thai, "Blaming the Victim," 305; Candy J. Cooper and Marc Aronson, *Poisoned Water: How the Citizens of Flint, Michigan, Fought for Their Lives and Warned the Nation* (Bloomsbury Children's Books, 2020).

141. Bullard, *Dumping in Dixie*.

142. Martine Vrijheid, "Health Effects of Residence Near Hazardous Waste Landfill Sites: A Review of Epidemiologic Literature," *Environmental Health Perspectives* 108, Suppl. 1 (2000). https://doi.org/10.2307/3454635.

143. American College of Obstetricians and Gynecologists, Committee on Obstetric Practice, "Committee Opinion No. 832: Reducing Prenatal Exposure to Toxic Environmental Agents," *Obstetrics and Gynecology* 138, no. 1 (July 2021), https://www.acog.org/Clinical/Clinical-Guidance/Committee-Opinion/Articles/2021/07/Reducing-Prenatal-Exposure-to-Toxic-Environmental-Agents.

144. Washington, *A Terrible Thing to Waste*.

145. Ibid.

146. Ibid.

147. Crystal Chavis, "Unhealthy and Home: The Lived Experiences of African Americans Impacted by Environmental Racism in the United States" (PhD diss., Nova Southeastern University, 2023).

148. Spencer Banzhaf, Lala Ma, and Christopher Timmins, "Environmental Justice: The Economics of Race, Place, and Pollution," *The Journal of Economic Perspectives* 33, no. 1 (2019): 185–208; Jason Corburn, "Concepts for Studying Urban Environmental Justice," *Current Environmental Health Reports* 4, no. 1 (2017).

149. Taylor, *Toxic Communities*.

150. Bullard, *Dumping in Dixie*.

151. Galtung, "Violence, Peace, and Peace Research."

152. Martin Luther King Jr., "Letter from a Birmingham Jail," April 16, 1963.

153. Taylor, *Toxic Communities*.

154. Darryl Fears, "Shingle Mountain: How a Pile of Toxic Pollution Was Dumped in a Community of Color," *Washington Post*, November 16, 2020, https://www.washingtonpost.com/climate-environment/2020/11/16/environmental-racism-dallas-shingle-mountain/.

155. Dallas Morning News, "Reckoning with Joppa: A Historic Freedman's Town Confronts Racism and Neglect," *The Dallas Morning News*, 2020, https://interactives.dallasnews.com/2020/historic-freedmans-town-joppa-confronts-history-racism-neglect-dallas/.

156. Eve Mayo, "A Case Study of Shingle Mountain, in Southern Dallas," Texas A&M University Hazard Reduction & Recovery Center, accessed December 4, 2025, https://mavmatrix.uta.edu/context/planning_reports/article/1013/type/native/viewcontent; Alejandra Martinez, "In the Shadow of 'Shingle Mountain,' Southeast Dallas Neighbors Fight to Dismantle a Legacy of Environmental Racism," *Texas Tribune*, December 9, 2020, https://www.texastribune.org/2020/12/09/southeast-dallas-shingle-mountain-environmental-racism/; "Residents Got Rid of Shingle Mountain. Is a Park in Their Future?" *Green Source DFW*, February 17, 2022, https://www.greensourcetexas.org/articles/residents-got-rid-shingle-mountain-park-their-future.

157. Marsha Jackson, interview by author, December 20, 2021.

158. City of Dallas Planning Department, "Zoning Map Amendments," 1985.

159. Jackson interview.

160. *City of Dallas v. Blue Star Recycling*, Case No. DC-18-18651 (2018).

161. "Toxic Waste Dumping in Shingle Mountain, Dallas, Texas," *Global Atlas of Environmental Justice*, last modified October 14, 2021, https://ejatlas.org/conflict/shingle-mountain.

162. Jackson, interview.

163. Ibid.

164. U.S. Environmental Protection Agency, *Health and Environmental Effects of Particulate Matter (PM)*, last modified May 23, 2025, https://www.epa.gov/pm-pollution/health-and-environmental-effects-particulate-matter-pm.

165. Wei Li et al., "A Review of Respirable Fine Particulate Matter (PM2.5)-Induced Brain Damage," *Frontiers in Molecular Neuroscience* 15 (2022), https://www.frontiersin.org/articles/10.3389/fnmol.2022.967174/full.

166. Modern Geosciences, LLC. *Blue Star Phase II Environmental Assessment.* Prepared for the City of Dallas, June 7, 2021. PDF, accessed December 7, 2025. https://drive.google.com/file/d/1K_y_jEGxLVgU-6_1E8eHXeWi4K-GrZmRN/view.

167. Jackson, interview.

168. Ibid.

169. U.S. Environmental Protection Agency, "Lead Regulator Policy for Cleanup Activities at Federal Facilities on the NPL," https://www.epa.gov/fedfac/lead-regulator-policy-cleanup-activities-federal-facilities-national-priorities-list.

170. Jackson, interview.

171. Robert Wilonsky, reporting series on Shingle Mountain, *Dallas Morning News*, 2018–2019.

172. *Disrupt & Dismantle*. "Shingle Mountain." Directed by Soledad O'Brien. Aired March 25, 2021, on BET.

173. Fears, "Shingle Mountain."

174. Matt Goodman, "The City Is Now Being Sued to Remove Shingle Mountain," *D Magazine*, July 24, 2020. https://www.dmagazine.com/frontburner/2020/07/the-city-is-now-being-sued-to-remove-shingle-mountain/.

175. FOX 4 Staff, "$450,000 deal being finalized to clean up 'Shingle Mountain' in Dallas," *FOX 4 News*, September 30, 2020. https://www.fox4news.com/news/450000-deal-being-finalized-to-clean-up-shingle-mountain-in-dallas.

176. Darryl Fears and John Muyskens, "Shingle Mountain: How a Pile of Toxic Waste Was Dumped in a Community of Color," *Washington Post*,

November 16, 2020. https://www.washingtonpost.com/climate-environment/2020/11/16/environmental-racism-dallas-shingle-mountain/.

177. Jerrold J. Heindel et al., "Environmental Epigenomics, Imprinting and Disease Susceptibility," *Epigenetics* 1, no. 1 (2006). https://doi.org/10.4161/epi.1.1.2642.

178. Heindel et al., "Environmental Epigenomics."

179. Southern Sector Rising. "Southern Sector Rising." Accessed December 7, 2025. https://southernsectorrising.org/.

180. City of Dallas, "Floral Farms (Z189-341)," Planning & Development – Authorized Hearing, accessed December 7, 2025, https://dallascityhall.com/departments/pnv/Pages/Floral-Farms.aspx

181. Jackson, interview.

182. Ibid.

183. Mona Hanna-Attisha, *What the Eyes Don't See: A Story of Crisis, Resistance, and Hope in an American City*. One World, 2018.

184. U.S. Census Bureau, *Number of Inhabitants: 1961*, in *Census of Population 1960, Volume I* (U.S. Department of Commerce, 1961), 24-12, https://www2.census.gov/library/publications/decennial/1960/population-volume-1/37722966v1p24ch2.pdf.

185. U.S. Census Bureau, 2020 census data, retrieved November 28, 2025, from https://www.census.gov/programs-surveys/decennial-census/decade.2020.html.

186. Sara Ganim and Linh Tran, "How Tap Water Became Toxic in Flint, Michigan," CNN, January 13, 2016, https://www.cnn.com/2016/01/11/health/toxic-tap-water-flint-michigan.

187. Cooper and Aronson, *Poisoned Water*.

188. Cooper and Aronson, *Poisoned Water*.

189. Ibid.

190. Michigan Department of Health and Human Services. "MDHHS Issues Update to 2015 Legionnaires' Disease Report for Genesee County," news release, April 11, 2016, https://www.michigan.gov/mdhhs/inside-mdhhs/newsroom/2016/04/11/mdhhs-issues-update-to-2015-legionnaires-disease-report-for-genesee-county_2;

ABC News, "3 Additional Cases Reported in Flint-Area Legionnaires' Outbreak," ABC News, April 12, 2016, https://abcnews.go.com/Health/additional-cases-reported-flint-area-legionnaires-outbreak/story?id=38345019.

191. Neilsberg Research, "Flint, MI Median Household Income: Trends, Analysis, and Key Findings," Neilsberg, https://www.neilsberg.com/insights/flint-mi-median-household-income/; Census Reporter, profile page for Flint, Genesee County, MI, 2023, https://censusreporter.org/profiles/06000US2604929000-flint-city-genesee-county-mi/.

192. Michigan Civil Rights Commission, *The Flint Water Crisis: Systemic Racism Through the Lens of Flint* (Michigan Department of Civil Rights, 2017), https://www.michigan.gov/-/media/Project/Websites/mdcr/mcrc/reports/2017/flint-crisis-report-edited.pdf.

193. Michigan Civil Rights Commission, *The Flint Water Crisis*; Michigan Civil Rights Commission, *Flint Water Crisis Study Guide* (Michigan De-

partment of Civil Rights, 2017), https://www.michigan.gov/-/media/Project/Websites/mdcr/racial-equity/studyguides/flint-water-crisis-study-guide.pdf?rev=45e185f720994a00afa4cd5077204c47.

194. Gale Malesky, "Update on Lead in Drinking Water: More Progress Needs to Be Made to Clean Up the Water," *Environmental Nutrition* 43, no. 6 (2020).

195. Cynthia Morris (pseudonym), interview by author, January 13, 2022.

196. Morris, interview.

197. Ibid.

198. Mona Hanna-Attisha et al., "Elevated Blood Lead Levels in Children Associated with the Flint Drinking Water Crisis: A Spatial Analysis of Risk and Public Health Response," *American Journal of Public Health* 106, no. 2 (2016).

199. Hanna-Attisha et al., "Elevated Blood Lead Levels."

200. Ibid.

201. Morris, interview.

202. Washington, *A Terrible Thing to Waste*.

203. Keith L. Bryant Jr., "Arthur E. Stilwell and the Founding of Port Arthur: A Case of Entrepreneurial Error," *Southwestern Historical Quarterly* 75, no. 1 (July 1971).

204. "Refining," Motiva Enterprises, accessed November 21, 2025, https://www.motiva.com/what-we-do/operations/refining.

205. John Beard Jr., interview by author, January 3, 2022.

206. Diane Jackson (pseudonym), interview by author, January 8, 2022.

207. Beard, interview.

208. Ibid.

209. Beard, interview.

210. Environmental Protection Agency (EPA), National Emissions Inventory Database, 2017.

211. Environmental Integrity Project. *Emissions and Enforcement in Texas: Annual Review of Industrial Air Pollution and Compliance*. 2020. https://environmentalintegrity.org.

212. U.S. Environmental Protection Agency, "New Source Review (NSR) Permitting," EPA.gov, accessed December 8, 2025, https://www.epa.gov/nsr.

213. Marcus Stern, Savanna Strott, and David Leffler, "Small Plant, Big Polluter," *Texas Observer*, November 2, 2021, https://www.texasobserver.org/small-plant-big-polluter/.

214. Stern et al., "Small Plant, Big Polluter."

215. Lone Star Legal Aid and Environmental Integrity Project. *Title VI Civil Rights Complaint Against Oxbow Calcining LLC*. Filed on behalf of Port Arthur Community Action Network, August 18, 2021. https://environmentalintegrity.org/wp-content/uploads/2021/08/2021.08.18_Oxbow-Title-VI-Complaint-Final.pdf.

216. Ibid.

217. U.S. Environmental Protection Agency, Office of External Civil Rights Compliance. *Administrative Closure of EPA Complaint No. 02R-21-R6*

(PACAN et al. v. Texas Commission on Environmental Quality / Oxbow Calcining, LLC). December 26, 2023.

218. Beard, interview.

219. Anne Robinson (pseudonym), interview by author, January 11, 2022.

220. Robinson, interview.

221. Beard, interview.

222. Ibid.

223. Ibid.

224. Ibid.

225. Ibid.

226. Ibid.

227. Ibid.

228. Beard, interview.

229. Ibid.

230. Beverly Wright, interview by John Yang, *PBS News Weekend*, PBS, September 7, 2024, https://www.pbs.org/newshour/show/what-a-court-ruling-means-for-the-future-of-pollution-in-louisianas-cancer-alley.

231. Paul W. Valentine, "Baltimore Targets Its High Rate of Illiteracy; Schmoke Pushing Programs to Make 'City That Reads' More Than Just an Idle Slogan," *Washington Post*, August 26, 1990, https://www.washingtonpost.com/archive/local/1990/08/27/baltimore-targets-its-high-rate-of-illiteracy/e2a171b8-4f4a-4c07-b354-eec90e959c63/; "The City That Reads: Novels

in Baltimore," Loyola Notre Dame Library, accessed November 19, 2025, https://loyolanotredamelib.org/CityThatReads/home.html.

232. Garrett Power, "Apartheid Baltimore Style: The Residential Segregation Ordinances of 1910–1913," *Maryland Law Review* 42, no. 2 (1983); "1910: Residential Segregation," The Baltimore Story: Learning and Living Racial Justice, accessed November 19, 2025, https://www.thebaltimorestory.org/history-1/1910-residential-segregation.

233. Lawrence T. Brown, *The Black Butterfly: The Harmful Politics of Race and Space in America*. Johns Hopkins University Press, 2021.

234. "Mapping Baybrook," Baltimore Traces, University of Maryland, Baltimore County, https://baltimoretraces.umbc.edu/mapping-baybrook/.

235. Carol Williams (pseudonym), interview by author, January 20, 2022.

236. Williams, interview.

237. Maryland Department of the Environment (MDE), *Title V Permit Renewal: Wheelabrator Baltimore Incinerator* (Baltimore, MD: MDE, 2020).

238. Ibid.

239. Environmental Integrity Project, "South Baltimore Advocates File Civil Rights Complaint Over Trash Incinerator Pollution Threats," May 29, 2024, https://environmentalintegrity.org/news/south-baltimore-advocates-file-civil-rights-complaint-over-trash-incinerator-pollution-threats/.

240. Ibid.

241. Williams, interview.

242. WIN Waste Innovations. "Waste-to-Energy Facility in Baltimore, MD." Accessed December 9, 2025. https://www.win-waste.com/about-us/locations/baltimore-md/.

243. "Incinerator Foes Sue Baltimore, but Young Prevails with 3–2 Vote for New Contract," *Baltimore Brew*, November 4, 2020, https://www.baltimorebrew.com/2020/11/04/incinerator-foes-sue-baltimore-but-young-prevails-with-3-2-vote-for-new-contract/.

244. Environmental Integrity Project, "South Baltimore Advocates File Civil Rights Complaint."

245. Ian Round, "Baltimore Mayor Signs New Clean Air Standards," *CNS Maryland*, March 20, 2019, https://cnsmaryland.org/2019/03/20/baltimore-mayor-signs-new-clean-air-standards/.

246. "B&D Wins Summary Judgment Ruling Voiding Baltimore Air Ordinance," Beveridge & Diamond PC, March 27, 2020, https://www.bdlaw.com/news/bd-wins-summary-judgment-ruling-voiding-baltimore-air-ordinance/.

247. Williams, interview.

248. Ibid.

249. "Attorney General Anthony Brown Announces Guilty Plea and Sentencing of Curtis Bay Energy, LP," Maryland Department of the Environment, October 17, 2023, https://news.maryland.gov/mde/2023/10/18/attorney-general-anthony-brown-announces-guilty-plea-and-sentencing-of-curtis-bay-energy-lp-owner-of-largest-medical-waste-incinerator-in-the-united-states/.

250. Jacob Wallace, "Curtis Bay Energy Fined $1.75M, Pleads Guilty to Improperly Incinerating Medical Waste," *Waste Dive*, October 18, 2023,

https://www.wastedive.com/news/curtis-bay-energy-medical-waste-incinerator-guilty-plea-baltimore-maryland/696945/.

251. Tess Kazdin, "Curtis Bay Energy Pleads Guilty to Improper Handling of Special Medical Waste," *Waste Today Magazine*, October 20, 2023, https://www.wastetodaymagazine.com/news/curtis-bay-energy-pleads-guilty-to-improper-handling-of-medical-waste/.

252. Fern Shen, "South Baltimore Medical Waste Incinerator Hit with a $1.75 Million State Fine and Penalty," *Baltimore Brew*, October 17, 2023, https://www.baltimorebrew.com/2023/10/17/south-baltimore-medical-waste-incinerator-hit-with-a-1-million-state-fine/.

253. Shen, "South Baltimore Medical Waste Incinerator."

254. Maryland Office of the Attorney General, "Attorney General Anthony Brown Announces Guilty Plea."

255. Tazdin, "Curtis Bay Energy Pleads Guilty."

256. Ibid.

257. *Baltimore Brew*, April 27, 2023. https://www.baltimorebrew.com/2023/04/27/pollution-from-the-bresco-incinerator-likely-to-continue-through-mid-2030s-city-report-says/.

258. "Health Damage: The Cost of Toxic Emissions," *Postindustrial*, July 29, 2025, https://postindustrial.com/stories/baltimore-incinerators-create-100-million-dollars-in-health-damage/.

259. Scott Maucione, "Baltimore Incinerators Cause About $100 Million in Health Costs, Study Says," WYPR, July 28, 2025, https://www.wypr.org/wypr-news/2025-07-28/baltimore-incinerators-cause-about-100-million-in-health-costs-study-says.

260. *2017 Neighborhood Health Profile: Citywide Overview.* Baltimore City Health Department, 2017. https://health.baltimorecity.gov/neighborhood-health-profile-reports.

261. Environmental Integrity Project, "South Baltimore Advocates File Civil Rights Complaint."

262. Williams, interview.

263. "Who Has to Obtain a Title V Permit?" U.S. Environmental Protection Agency, last updated August 7, 2025, https://www.epa.gov/title-v-operating-permits/who-has-obtain-title-v-permit; "CAA Permitting in Maryland," U.S. Environmental Protection Agency, last updated June 30, 2025, https://www.epa.gov/caa-permitting/caa-permitting-maryland.

264. "Incinerator Foes Sue Baltimore," *Baltimore Brew*.

265. South Baltimore Community Land Trust et al., *Title VI Complaint* (2024).

266. *Comcast Corp. v. National Association of African American-Owned Media et al.*, 140 S. Ct. 1009 (2020), https://www.supremecourt.gov/opinions/19pdf/18-1171_4425.pdf.

267. Title VI of the Civil Rights Act of 1964, 42 U.S.C. § 2000d et seq.

268. Jacob Wallace, "EPA Opens Civil Rights Investigation into Baltimore Waste Plan," *Waste Dive*, July 17, 2024, https://www.wastedive.com/news/epa-opens-civil-rights-investigation-into-baltimore-waste-plan/721575/.

269. Williams, interview.

270. Ibid.

271. Ibid.

272. Williams, interview.

273. Ibid.

274. Ibid.

275. Greta Thunberg, speech delivered at the 24th Conference of the Parties to the United Nations Framework Convention on Climate Change (COP24), December 2018.

276. Benjamin F. Chavis Jr., "The Historical Significance and Challenges of the First National People of Color Environmental Leadership Summit," in *Proceedings of the First National People of Color Environmental Leadership Summit* (United Church of Christ, Commission for Racial Justice, 1992), 8.

277. Bullard, *Dumping in Dixie*; U.S. Environmental Protection Agency, "EPA Launches New National Office."

278. United Church of Christ, *Toxic Wastes and Race in the United States*.

279. Ibid.

280. U.S. Environmental Protection Agency, *Environmental Equity: Reducing Risk for All Communities* (U.S. Environmental Protection Agency, June 1992).

281. Bullard, *Dumping in Dixie*.

282. Bullard et al., *Toxic Wastes and Race at Twenty*.

283. United Church of Christ, Commission for Racial Justice, *Proceedings: The First National People of Color Environmental Leadership Summit* (United Church of Christ, 1992).

284. Bullard, *The Quest for Environmental Justice*, 19–22.

285. United Church of Christ, *Proceedings*, xiii–xiv.

286. U.S. Environmental Protection Agency, *Towards an Environmental Justice Collaborative Model* (U.S. Environmental Protection Agency, 2003), https://www.epa.gov/sites/default/files/2015-09/documents/towards-ej-collaborative-model-evaluation.pdf.

287. U.S. Environmental Protection Agency, *EJSCREEN Fact Sheet*, July 2016, https://www.epa.gov/sites/default/files/2016-07/documents/ejscreen_fact_sheet.pdf.

288. Bullard and Wright, *Race, Place, and Environmental Justice*.

289. "About the National Environmental Justice Advisory Council," U.S. Environmental Protection Agency, accessed November 28, 2025, https://www.epa.gov/faca/about-national-environmental-justice-advisory-council.

290. "NEJAC Membership," U.S. Environmental Protection Agency, accessed October 29, 2025, https://www.epa.gov/faca/nejac-membership.

291. Environmental Justice Act of 1992, S. 2806, 102d Cong. (1992); H.R. 5326, 102d Cong. (1992).

292. Exec. Order No. 12898.

293. Luke W. Cole and Sheila R. Foster, *From the Ground Up: Environmental Racism and the Rise of the Environmental Justice Movement*. New York University Press, 2001.

294. Robert D. Bullard et al., eds., *Environmental Health and Racial Equity in the United States: Building Environmentally Just, Sustainable, and Livable Communities*. APHA Press, 2011.

295. "Environmental Justice Program," California Environmental Protection Agency (CalEPA), accessed October 30, 2025, https://calepa.ca.gov/envjustice/.

296. New Jersey Environmental Justice Law of 2020, P.L.2020, c.92.

297. Louisiana Bucket Brigade, "Pollution Tools + Resources," accessed October 2025, https://labucketbrigade.org/pollution-tools-resources/; North Carolina Environmental Justice Network, Home Page, accessed October 30, 2025, https://ncejn.org/.

298. "About Us," Port Arthur Community Action Network (PACAN), accessed October 2025, https://www.portarthurcan.org/index.html; "About Us," Texas Environmental Justice Advocacy Services (t.e.j.a.s.), accessed October 30, 2025, https://tejasbarrios.org/principles.

299. New York City Mayor's Office of Climate & Environmental Justice, *AdaptNYC: The City of New York's Strategic Climate Plan* (2024), https://climate.cityofnewyork.us; City of Los Angeles, *LA's Green New Deal: Sustainability pLAn 2019* (updated 2021), https://plan.lamayor.org; City of Seattle Office of Sustainability & Environment, *Resilience Hubs Planning Framework* (2022), https://www.seattle.gov/environment.

300. Barbara A. Israel et al., eds., *Methods in Community-Based Participatory Research for Health*, 2nd ed. Jossey-Bass, 2013.

301. "About Us," Deep South Center for Environmental Justice, accessed October 30, 2025, https://dscej.org/about/; "How We Work," Bullard Center for Environmental and Climate Justice at Texas Southern University, accessed November 20, 2025, https://www.bullardcenter.org/about/how-we-work; University of Michigan School for Environment and Sustainability, *Environmental Justice Program*, accessed October 2025, https://seas.umich.edu/academics/master-science/environmental-justice.

302. Bullard et al., *Toxic Wastes and Race at Twenty*.

303. United Church of Christ, *Toxic Wastes and Race in the United States*.

304. Bullard et al., *Toxic Wastes and Race at Twenty*.

305. U.S. Environmental Protection Agency, "Study Finds Exposure to Air Pollution Higher for People of Color Regardless of Region or Income," September 20, 2021, https://www.epa.gov/sciencematters/study-finds-exposure-air-pollution-higher-people-color-regardless-region-or-income.

306. Christopher W. Tessum et al., "Inequity in Consumption of Goods and Services Adds to Racial–Ethnic Disparities in Air Pollution Exposure," *Proceedings of the National Academy of Sciences* 116, no. 13 (2019).

307. Bullard and Wright, *The Wrong Complexion for Protection*.

308. Executive Order No. 14008, "*Tackling the Climate Crisis at Home and Abroad*," *Federal Register* 86, no. 19 (February 1, 2021), https://www.federalregister.gov/documents/2021/02/01/2021-02177/tackling-the-climate-crisis-at-home-and-abroad.

309. U.S. Environmental Protection Agency, "EPA Launches New National Office Dedicated to Advancing Environmental Justice and Civil Rights," news release, September 24, 2022, https://www.epa.gov/newsreleases/epa-launches-new-national-office-dedicated-advancing-environmental-justice-and-civil.

310. Catherine Coleman Flowers, *Holy Ground: On Activism, Environmental Justice, and Finding Hope* (Spiegel and Grau, 2025).

311. Bullard, *Dumping in Dixie*.

312. Taylor, *Toxic Communities*.

313. Bullard and Wright, *The Wrong Complexion for Protection*.

314. U.S. Environmental Protection Agency, *EJScreen Technical Documentation, Version 2.3* (Washington, DC: EPA, updated July 31, 2024), https://www.

epa.gov/system/files/documents/2024-07/ejscreen-tech-doc-version-2-3.pdf; Bullard, *Dumping in Dixie*; Ellen Griffith Spears, *Baptized in PCBs: Race, Pollution, and Justice in an All-American Town*. Chapel Hill: University of North Carolina Press, 2014.

315. Dick Kasperowski et al., "Where Environmental Citizen Science Meets the Law," *Citizen Science: Theory and Practice* 8, no. 1 (2023), https://doi.org/10.5334/cstp.596.

316. *Bean v. Southwestern Waste Management Corp.*, 482 F. Supp. 673 (S.D. Tex. 1979).

317. Paul Mohai and Bunyan Bryant, "Environmental Racism: Reviewing the Evidence," in *Race and the Incidence of Environmental Hazards, eds. Bunyan Bryant and Paul Mohai* (Westview Press, 1992).

318. Barbara A. Israel et al., "Review of Community-Based Research: Assessing Partnership Approaches to Improve Public Health," *Annual Review of Public Health* 19 (1998), https://doi.org/10.1146/annurev.publhealth.19.1.173.

319. Sacoby M. Wilson, Devon C. Payne-Sturges, and L. Ebony Johnson Thornton, "A Critical Review of an Authentic and Transformative Environmental Justice and Health Community–University Partnership," *International Journal of Environmental Research and Public Health* 11, no. 12 (2014), https://doi.org/10.3390/ijerph111212817; University of Maryland School of Public Health, "Sacoby Wilson," accessed December 9, 2025, https://sph.umd.edu/people/sacoby-wilson; "About Us," Center for Community Engagement, Environmental Justice and Health, accessed November 28, 2025, https://ceejh.org/about-us/.

320. Dorceta E. Taylor, *Diversity in Environmental Organizations: Reporting and Transparency, Report 1* (University of Michigan, School for Environment and Sustainability, 2018).

321. Catherine Coleman Flowers, *Waste: One Woman's Fight Against America's Dirty Secret* (The New Press, 2020).

322. Naomi Klein, *This Changes Everything: Capitalism vs. the Climate* (Simon & Schuster, 2014).

323. United Nations, *Sustainable Development Goals Report* (United Nations Publications, 2023).

324. United Nations, *Sustainable Development Goals*.

325. Bullard et al., *Toxic Wastes and Race at Twenty*.

326. Wright and Bullard, *The Wrong Complexion for Protection*.

327. *Alexander v. Sandoval*, 532 U.S. 275 (2001).

328. Bullard, *Dumping in Dixie*.

329. John Lewis, remarks from the Edmund Pettus Bridge in Selma, Alabama, March 1, 2020.

330. Michael K. Honey, *Going Down Jericho Road: The Memphis Strike, Martin Luther King's Last Campaign* (W.W. Norton and Company, 2007); Frank Bardacke, *Trampling Out the Vintage: Cesar Chavez and the Two Souls of the United Farm Workers* (Verso, 2011).

331. Dorceta E. Taylor, *The Rise of the American Conservation Movement: Power, Privilege, and Environmental Protection* (Duke University Press, 2016).

332. Taylor, *Toxic Communities*; Hanna-Attisha, *What the Eyes Don't See*; Flowers, *Waste*; Wright and Bullard, *Race, Place, and the Environment After Hurricane Katrina*; Ali, "About Mustafa."

333. Wangari Maathai, *The Green Belt Movement: Sharing the Approach and the Experience* (Lantern Books, 2003).

334. Vann R. Newkirk II, "Trump's EPA Concludes Environmental Racism Is Real," *The Atlantic*, February 28, 2018, https://www.theatlantic.com/politics/archive/2018/02/the-trump-administration-finds-that-environmental-racism-is-real/554315/.

335. "Environmental and Climate Justice," NAACP, accessed November 20, 2025, https://naacp.org/know-issues/environmental-climate-justice; GreenLatinos, home page, accessed November 20, 2025, https://www.greenlatinos.org/; WE ACT for Environmental Justice, home page, accessed October 30, 2025, https://weact.org/; Indigenous Environmental Network, home page, accessed October 30, 2025, https://www.ienearth.org/; Earthjustice, home page, accessed October 30, 2025, https://earthjustice.org.

336. Gaige Hunter Kerr et al., "Increasing Racial and Ethnic Disparities in Ambient Air Pollution–Attributable Morbidity and Mortality in the United States," *Environmental Health Perspectives* 132, no. 3 (2024); NIHCM Foundation, "Environmental Health: Air Pollution, COVID-19 & Health Disparities," webinar (August 21, 2020), https://nihcm.org/publications/environmental-health-air-pollution-covid-19-health-disparities.

337. "Justice40: A Whole-of-Government Initiative," White House, accessed November 21, 2025, https://bidenwhitehouse.archives.gov/environmental-justice/justice40/.

338. "Trump Rescinded Biden's Executive Order 14008 Establishing Justice40 Initiative," Federal Environmental Justice Tracker, Harvard Law School, last updated March 1, 2025, https://eelp.law.harvard.edu/tracker/rollback-trump-rescinded-bidens-executive-order-14008-that-established-justice40-initiative/; Exec. Order No. 14148, "Initial Rescissions of Harmful Executive Orders and Actions," *Federal Register* 90, no. 17 (Jan. 28, 2025), https://www.govinfo.gov/content/pkg/FR-2025-01-28/pdf/2025-01901.pdf.

339. *Loper Bright Enterprises v. Raimondo*, 603 U.S. 369 (2024).

340. U.S. Environmental Protection Agency (EPA), "EPA Proposes Repeal of Biden-Harris EPA Regulations for Power Plants," press release, June 11, 2025.

341. Gavin Maguire, "U.S. Clean Power Reversal Comes with a Hefty Emissions Price Tag," *Reuters*, October 15, 2025), https://www.reuters.com/business/energy/us-clean-power-reversal-comes-with-hefty-emissions-price-tag-2025-10-15/.

342. GAO, *Environmental Justice*; EPA, *Enforcement Annual Results*; Bullard and Wright, *Wrong Complexion for Protection*.

343. EPA, *EJScreen Technical Documentation*; Union of Concerned Scientists, *Cumulative Impacts: Recommendations for the Environmental Protection Agency*, submitted to the National Environmental Justice Advisory Council (NEJAC), 2022, https://www.ucs.org/resources/cumulative-impacts-recommendations-epa; Gretchen T. Goldman et al., "Ensuring Scientific Integrity in the Age of Trump," *Science* 355, no. 6326 (2017), https://pubmed.ncbi.nlm.nih.gov/28209862/.

www.ingramcontent.com/pod-product-compliance
Lightning Source LLC
Chambersburg PA
CBHW020543030426
42337CB00013B/959